LIFE AS A JIGSAW PUZZLE

LIFE AS A JIGSAW PUZZLE

A little book about **LOVE**

HANH TAT

ISBN: 978-1-7394626-0-4
eBook ISBN: 978-1-7394626-1-1
First Edition: 2023

A catalogue record for this book is available from the British Library.

For inquiries regarding permissions, please contact Hanh Tat:
contact@hanhtat.com
www.hanhtat.com

To my dearest Elliot and Blake. My deepest hope is that by the time you are able to read this book with complete comprehension of its contents, you'll be left in no doubt that you are truly and unconditionally loved.

CONTENTS

INTRODUCTION

Sometimes, when I'm on the cusp of wakefulness yet my mind is still lingering in the dreaminess of slumber, and I have been blessed with time, I like to allow myself the luxury of letting my mind wander and observing what thoughts arise. It's an enjoyable pastime which often reveals helpful insights or reflections that I am able to incorporate into my life.

One morning, during one of these cognitive jam sessions, I recalled a random musing that I'd had previously on the fact that I like puzzles because I like finding solutions. I reflected on how I particularly like jigsaw puzzles because of how the picture builds up piece by piece towards completion.

My thoughts meandered to thinking about how life is like a jigsaw puzzle, but one where we don't have the box so we don't know what the completed picture is supposed to look like. And, in turn, one where we won't know how it will look until just before the end of our given life.

This jigsaw puzzle of ours is made up of billions of pieces, each representing a decision we made or an action we took and one that builds up as the different parts of our lives evolve and take shape. It's one where seemingly random disconnected pieces eventually join up and fit together to reveal a complete section of the full picture. And often these sections take forms which we could never have envisaged until we had found all the necessary pieces.

I also thought about how this last aspect reflects real life, how when seemingly unconnected events happen and you find yourself wondering what the point of each of them was. But how if you are patient, accepting, have faith and wait long enough, you realise that each event was necessary to lead you to a given outcome or learning. And from these learnings, you are ultimately led to your own inner growth.

I went on to wonder whether the picture is static, being the same from the very first puzzle piece of when you're born, right to the very last piece when you pass, as I guess it would be if you believe in predeterminism (the philosophy that all events, past, present and future, have already been established). Or would it be continually morphing, as you'd expect if you believe in free will and the ability to control our own destinies through personal choice?

The topic of predeterminism versus free will has been widely debated over centuries but I personally don't feel compelled to choose one over the other. My preference is to be fascinated by the theories and opinions on both sides, whilst settling somewhere between the two, depending on which best serves me in a given moment. For instance, when adverse events occur that are outside of our control, it's more helpful for our mental and emotional health to accept that some things cannot be affected by our free will, thus freeing us from rumination and anguish. Yet at other times, knowing that we have free will and therefore agency to determine how things will impact us provides the capacity to not fall foul of victimhood in the face of adversities.

But either way, predeterminism or free will prevailing, it got me thinking about how this could be applied to our lives. Maybe the point of life is to build up our individual jigsaw puzzles, piece by piece, section by section, into a final picture that we're happy with. And what if we were to do this whilst simultaneously embracing the uncertainty of life? How would we be impacted by understanding that we're not going to know how the whole puzzle fits together or what the final picture will look like until right at the end of our time? Would that help us to be okay with that concept and just embrace that uncertainty? Or rather than being just okay with the uncertainty, what would happen if we saw it as a gift, as an opportunity to actively cultivate a curiosity and excitement about what the final picture will be?

If we have the grace to accept and be at peace with the fact that we won't know how the complete jigsaw puzzle will look until the final bell, we can live our lives less in fear of the unknown. We could be less daunted by that uncertainty which often clouds our thinking and perceptions of events in our lives, and can cause us to behave in ways that are not in our highest good.

I also wondered how we would be represented in the jigsaw puzzles of other people in our lives. Would it be from their perspectives of us, seen through their unique lenses, and if so, would that differ greatly from how we imagine ourselves to appear? And would it differ from how we appear on our own jigsaw puzzles?

And what about the sides? Would there be four, as with traditional jigsaw puzzles, or multiple edges, reflecting the different facets of our being?

It occurred to me that maybe all our individual puzzles somehow amalgamate into one infinite glorious masterpiece for the whole of creation. And how the more beautifully we can cultivate our own individual versions, the more resplendent the collective picture becomes.

If we take the time to step back from the hustle and bustle of our modern lives to ponder on how we want our own jigsaw puzzle to unfold, what would we want the final completed picture to look like? What would we envisage? If we were to do this in addition to assessing how we want to be represented on the jigsaw puzzles of others, we could then consider each of the areas that make up our lives and make conscious decisions about how we are going to curate them.

Sometimes in life, when we're caught up in the busyness of it all, it's the simple and obvious things, which should be common sense and common knowledge, that get easily forgotten or overlooked due to their obviousness and simplicity. One such noteworthy thing is the fact that, ultimately, our lives are made up of how we live each individual day and the moments within those days. And that if we can smile at our reflection when we wake up, happy with the person we are or are intending to be; if we can put our heads down to sleep at the end of the day, happy with the person we've been that given day; and if we can do this consistently throughout our lives, then we can create a final jigsaw puzzle picture to be joyful about.

CHAPTER 1

LOVE

In considering the areas in our lives that make up our complete jigsaw puzzle picture, I will start off with the subject of love because I believe that this is the common thread that weaves throughout the entire tapestry of our lives. It is the thing which connects all of the other areas, from our relationships in all their forms (familial, romantic, platonic and so forth) to our careers and our health.

When we talk about love, due to social conditioning through the prevalence of romantic movies and novels, it's common for people to assume that we're talking about romantic love. A quick internet search using the phrase, 'What is love?' supports this, returning nearly thirty results on romantic love before the first article on love as a general subject appears. Now don't get me wrong, I am as much of a fan of romantic love as the next person; that euphoric high of the dopamine hits when you meet someone new can be hard to resist. But love is infinitely more expanded and all-encompassing than being merely about romantic love, and to confine it to such would be to do ourselves a great disservice as humans.

So it's imperative that we broaden our scope on how we think of love in order to receive the boundless gifts that it offers. Therefore, when I write about love throughout this book, I'm referring to it in its broadest terms possible, from love for ourselves, our loved ones, people we know and even those we don't know, right through to our beloved planet. And hopefully what I mean by this will all fit together by the time you reach the final page of this book.

I think clarity around the definition of love is also needed at this juncture. Love has always fascinated humankind throughout the ages, and tomes upon tomes have been written on the subject, and yet a clear definition still remains elusive, as intangible and subjective as it is by nature. It's hard to say with one hundred per cent clarity what love actually is because it's not a thing that we can touch and hold. And what it means to me may be very different to what it means to you.

Some people say that love is a feeling, and that makes sense and is helpful - to an extent. It's easy to know how love feels when we think of our loved ones (significant other, family, friends) and people we like. But what about when it comes to people outside of this circle, such as challenging co-workers, shop assistants and even strangers we see walking down the street? I'd hazard a guess that most people would say that they don't feel love for these people. So from this definition and perspective, love is very limited.

But what if we were to think of love as a way of being, and to see it as an umbrella term for all the other loving ways of being, such as kindness, compassion, patience, gentleness, acceptance and forgiveness? Could we then offer love to people outside of our circle of loved ones? Or be gentler with our co-workers if meetings get a little heated? Could we be more patient with the shop assistant if they're short with us because they're having a tough day? Or offer a smile to that person we pass on the street, even if they don't reciprocate? In the remainder of this book, I will use love as this umbrella term just described.

It might not seem obvious but by choosing our behaviours consciously in these little ways, we're showing love to others and without our knowing, by doing so we create ripple effects that cascade out. Our co-workers are less stressed at the end of the meeting and, in turn, are gentler with others. The shop assistant is a little happier (or less unhappy) in their job so is able to cope better. The stranger on the street might themselves think to smile at another passer-by that they come across, which could help lift their mood.

In writing this book, there have been times when defeatism arose, when the fear of opening myself up (as revealed in later chapters) to all and sundry led me to question my own motives, *What's the point? It won't make any difference, nobody's going to read it anyway.* During the times when these fears surfaced, I counselled myself that if I can use my journey through adversity and what it taught me to help others navigate their own lives more easily, then it won't have been for nothing, and even if only one person was to benefit from reading my story, then I will have made a difference. It was love, in the form of wanting to be of service to others, that propelled me to start writing this book in the first instance, and it has been that same love that has sustained me during its unfolding when self-doubt made its occasional appearance. So you see, love can take many guises and thus in order to appreciate its full power, we need to broaden our definition to encompass all acts of kindness.

And why is this important? It all goes back to that final jigsaw puzzle picture and how we want it to look when it's complete.

What are the important things that we want to appear in the end, and what are the aspects which may seem significant at the time but in the grand scheme of our lives really don't matter? Next time you find yourself in an argument or in conflict with someone, take a brief moment to consider whether that argument/conflict will have any meaning when that complete picture is finally revealed to you, or whether you even want it to feature.

Now, I'm not saying that we should become doormats to be trampled over in order to avoid conflict at all costs - no, not at all, but simply that we have a choice, even in times of conflict. We can choose to be more loving, use kinder words and express ourselves in a gentler, less aggressive, less confrontational way at any given moment and in all situations. It is possible to do all of these things whilst still standing firm on what we believe in, without compromising our integrity. Non-violent communication is possible where conflict arises. And if we approach conflict from a loving perspective, it can become an opportunity to collaborate and collectively find a creative solution, rather than necessarily leading to animosity.

And neither am I saying that it's always easy, not by any stretch, but simply that it's possible if we make it our intention and put effort into applying that intention. And the more we try, the easier it should become, and the easier it becomes, the more we'll end up doing it until we eventually find ourselves doing it without effort. And the more people that take up and apply this intention to be more loving, kinder and gentler, the less conflict there will be within homes. And if there is less conflict within homes, there will be less conflict within communities, and if there is less conflict within communities, there will be less conflict within towns and cities. You see where I'm going with this, right?

I am aware that this might sound naive, unrealistic and utopian-like thinking, but everything that has ever been created in the world started off with the belief in its possibility. And thus we shouldn't let scepticism or cynicism lull us into apathy and complacency. I believe that there are a great many people on the planet with a desire for a more loving and kinder world, and that desire can be harnessed to create change for the better.

It might take a very long time, possibly exceeding a lifetime. But if we start to sow the seeds now, firstly by becoming conscious of our own thoughts and behaviours, and instilling that desire in the children in our lives, then eventually at some point, generations down the line will be able to harvest the seeds sown in our lifetimes, and will inherit a more tolerant and peaceful world.

If nobody does anything because they don't believe it will make a difference, then nothing changes. But if everybody was to make an effort, even a small one, in the hope that it will make a difference, no matter how seemingly insignificant, then we have at least a chance of effecting positive change, even if that change won't be visible in our lifetimes.

If we as individuals take personal responsibility for our own behaviour, the ripple effect spreads and if enough of us do it, we create a critical mass from which the effect proliferates exponentially. Or at least that's what I think and hope is possible. Just think what a magnificent collective jigsaw puzzle picture we could contribute to if we took up this action.

If we can teach our children/the next generations to live in a more loving, tolerant, compassionate and kinder way, through the role modelling of our own words, actions and behaviours, in time to come we will create a kinder and more loving world. What parent/grandparent or other adult with children in their

9

lives wouldn't want this for those children? Most of the parents I know already possess a great sense of responsibility over their roles as parents and are already doing a grand job of raising their offspring. And as a parent myself, I know how difficult this can get, especially when faced with modern challenges which weren't around in our parents' day (mostly as a consequence of technological advancements).

But even as I'm writing this book, eulogising the fostering of more loving attitudes and behaviours towards others, I often find myself getting frustrated by the antics of my two sometimes raucous, rambunctious and testing boys. And it's at times when they're playing up that I could very easily succumb to my frustrations and behave in less-than-loving ways. But I try to use these occurrences as opportunities to practise patience, to take a step back and hold my bigger jigsaw puzzle picture in my periphery. This affords me a brief moment to consciously choose a more loving response, rather than reacting impulsively based on my conditioning and emotions.

Again, I'm not saying that doing this is easy, or that I always get it right, especially on days when my hormones seem to be in charge and I can't work out why I'm feeling so irritable (I am in the throes of perimenopause). But if I do find that I've snapped at my boys unjustifiably, I will always practise the 'rupture and repair' process afterwards to make amends for the conflict in order to strengthen my bond with them.[1]

So for those of us who are parents, we are in the privileged position of shaping the adults of the future and we have a great

---

[1] Rupture and repair is a process used in psychotherapy to strengthen relationships. Put simply, after a conflict has arisen within a relationship (the rupture), the parties involved take steps to make amends and learn from the conflict, in order to better understand each other and avoid future repetition (repair).

duty to be mindful of what we teach our children, in both our verbal and non-verbal communications with them. Sometimes, as parents, it's easy to fall into the trap of, 'do as I say, not as I do,' but often it's what we do that our children will pick up on; it's how we live our own lives that will influence the minds and emotions of our precious little ones. We need to exhibit the behaviours that we want our children to adopt, not simply order them to follow instructions without doing so ourselves. Love calls us to parent more consciously[2] and in doing so, we not only cultivate a more radiant jigsaw puzzle for ourselves, we also teach our children to do so for themselves.

But children aside, I can't imagine there's a human alive, parent or not, who wouldn't want to grow old in a more loving and kinder world. But this won't come about on its own, just by virtue of a desire for it to be so - it's up to each and every one of us to play our part in creating a future that we want to see. When we think of the magnitude of our planet, it's easy to feel insignificant and succumb to perceptions of the futility of our own individual actions. But as expressed in multiple teachings, seas and oceans are made up of droplets of water and vast deserts, grains of sand. Our individual actions matter: they ripple out and impact those in our lives, and all the individual ripples make up a swell of consciousness that collectively has the power to change the way we live our lives for the better.

Whilst I'm not so naive to think that the world's problems will be solved or that any individual's life circumstances will necessarily be dramatically improved just by us all being a bit nicer to each other, I do believe that it can help us get more out of our day-to-day lives if we are. There are a great many things

---

[2] You can search the internet for *conscious parenting* for a plethora of useful resources.

in our lives and this world of ours that are beyond our realms of influence, and they will still be present whether we are kinder to each other or not. So given that this is the case, would it not assist us and those around us if we became more present and consciously chose to be more loving and kinder to one another?

If it is true that we have the ability and power to choose what appears on the final completed masterpiece, would it not be preferable to choose a more inspired, empowered and loving course of action wherever possible, especially during times of conflict?

They say that beauty is within the eye of the beholder, and whilst this may be true when viewed through judgemental and critical eyes, when viewed through loving eyes, beauty becomes universal. But we're not conditioned to see the beauty in everything due to our brains' negativity bias. So to see the beauty in everything doesn't always come easily for us all, but it is something that can be learnt should we choose to do so; it can be something that we nurture, something we can practise until it becomes our default, our norm.

And why would we want to do this? Put in the most basic of terms, because life is a gift. This simple yet empowering perspective gets easily and often forgotten in the midst of the rigmarole of daily life. I write this as much as a reminder for myself as anything, because sometimes the challenges of modern-day parenting, with daily battles over screen time and the temptations of abundant junk food availability, can become overwhelming, especially as a single parent, and so I know how it feels to find myself caught in the mire of frustration. Being both nurturer and disciplinarian is not an easy balance to get right for the parent and can be confusing for the children. That's not to say it's impossible, simply that it requires extra effort, focus, patience and creativity.

Reminding myself to see life as a gift, and each moment as an opportunity to practise patience and loving kindness helps lift the responsibility of parenting from being laborious to a blessing to be grateful for, in the knowledge that the effort is worthwhile.

Do I still get frustrated with my boys at times? Yes. Do I still lose my temper with them at times? Yes, because I am human. But do they know I love them deeply? Yes. Even when I'm teaching them about healthy boundaries, they know that it comes from a place of love and not one of control. They might not always like it, but that comes with the territory and I'm hoping that in time, they'll be able to create their own beautiful jigsaw puzzles.

And if my focus seems weighted towards being a parent, that's because it's a significant part of my life. But love in its broadest terms and broadest definition, and the application of love in our lives, is universally relevant for all sentient beings in contributing to a richer life experience.

To consciously integrate love into our daily lives will help us curate our final jigsaw puzzle pictures into personal masterpieces. And circularly, in learning to keep our final picture in mind throughout our lives, we are assisted in that cultivation. And as our personal jigsaw puzzles build up masterfully, so does the collective universal jigsaw puzzle of which we are a part.

CHAPTER 2

SELF-LOVE

Before I start this chapter, it's important to state that when talking about self-love, I am referring to healthy, non-narcissistic love and care for oneself. As per the previous chapter on *Love*, my definition of self-love encompasses the broadest definition of love, including self-compassion, self-acceptance and all forms of loving kindness towards oneself.

Love starts with self-love. Growing up, the concept of self-love was not well known, if at all, but nowadays it is commonplace in the wellness space and widely discussed and taught. Despite this though, I think it's something that we Brits aren't as comfortable talking about as our American cousins across the pond.

In Britain, I think it's fair to say that talking about love still feels corny or cheesy to many, especially of my generation and older, and discussing self-love even more so. In fact, when I first heard the term 'self-love' several years ago, I didn't pay it much interest because I thought it sounded narcissistic or egotistical, and thus counter to my parents' Buddhist mentality and my humble and modest upbringing. But thankfully perceptions are starting to change, especially with the growing body of teachings that has emerged around the subject. And upon learning more about it myself, I realised the inaccuracy of my initial assumptions.

In February 2020, I experienced a life-changing heartbreak when my husband, whom I'd been with for over 12 years and is the father of my two children, and I split up. At the time, it felt like my world as I perceived it was no more and I felt emotions that I'd never experienced before, of an intensity that I never imagined possible. The word 'heartbreak' is very apt because, at times, it felt like that could physically happen. This propelled me into a quest to mend my broken heart, which I go into in detail in later chapters.

And it was through starting to do the inner work to heal my heart from the end of my marriage that I started to learn about self-love. There's an old saying along the lines of, 'The teacher is always there, but the student only truly learns when they are ready,' and unlike the first time I'd come across the phrase 'self-love', this time I was ready and receptive and it opened up a whole world for me to study.

For the benefit of anyone new to the concept of inner work, in a nutshell, this encompasses the practice of focussing our attention away from our external world, towards our internal landscape. We explore our thoughts and our emotions in order to understand ourselves and why we are the way we are, and make any necessary changes to enable us to become better, happier, fuller versions of ourselves. It is a vast subject with more teachings than could fit in your local library, but more on this later.

This book isn't meant to be a manual on inner work and thus makes no attempt to provide guidance on it other than to extoll its importance for all of us as human beings. In the appendix, I have listed some of the resources that I found useful, but inner work is as personal to each of us as we are unique. The methods that work for one individual might be less effective for another, and the best way to ascertain levels of efficacy of different modalities is to learn about them and try them for yourselves.

For many things in life, there is no better teacher than direct experience. That's how it was for me. Every time I learnt about a new modality, I gave it a go and worked out whether it resonated with me or not. On the whole, the practices I've stuck with have been the ones that emerged as supportive during my experimentation, but there have also been some techniques that I didn't gel with on the first try that I have revisited, to see if subsequent attempts felt any different.

But now, let's go back to self-love. Once I started learning about it, I quickly realised that whilst I had a strong sense of self-worth, when I reflected back on my life, it became clear to me that I actually didn't have as much self-love as I thought I had. Often, ignorance makes us blind to things that subsequent education shines a light on, allowing us to see those things that were previously hidden from us.

When we gain new knowledge and insights and apply them in the context of our own lives, they can reveal to us things we hadn't seen previously. And when we are able to incorporate our newly expanded awareness into our lives, it's akin to finding pieces of our jigsaw puzzle that we didn't know existed.

During my education, I was a typical studious Asian (my family and I are Chinese), I worked hard and was a high achiever. With this came a level of perfectionism and fear of failure that caused me to get really annoyed with myself if I got things wrong and compelled me to push myself academically to the point of constant self-imposed stress and anxiety.

This carried into my career where even though I was successful, if I ever felt like I hadn't done or said things quite right, or had made little mistakes, this would leave me frustrated with myself and I would overanalyse situations and think about how I should have done better. And I frequently judged myself harshly - I was stereotypically my own worst critic.

My perfectionistic tendencies drove me to strive and push myself to do my best and be my best in all areas of my life. Coupled with being brought up to always be helpful, I was a do-it-all woman.

In my marriage, I was a dutiful wife and mother whilst earning as much as my then-husband (despite working part-time) and contributing equally to the family finances. I took my role and responsibilities seriously, carrying them out with vigour and diligence. I did the lion's share of the housework during the week so that we could have family time on the weekends. And I did more of the school runs to make it easier for my husband who worked full-time. After an argument, I would assess the cause, try to work out where we'd gone wrong and suggest ways to avoid the same mistake in future. When I sensed distance between my spouse and myself in the final stages, I tried to close it. I even got involved in DIY, not seeing why this should be the domain of the man of the house. I worked hard and did all the things I thought I should have done to make life easier and better for my family and to make my marriage a success.

So unsurprisingly, its eventual failure hit me with a sledgehammer-like force. I was dumbfounded as to how it had come about and I couldn't help trying to analyse where it had gone wrong and whether I could have done more to avoid it happening.

Even with my marriage ending, I questioned and blamed myself for contributing to its demise. Should I have been better at asking for help, rather than being a martyr and taking on everything myself and then becoming resentful at the imbalance in the partnership? Should I have shown more vulnerability and allowed my softer, gentler side more room, rather than staying in my more masculine, strong alpha-female persona so much?

After acquiring my newfound knowledge of self-love, I used it to reflect back on my own life and this enabled me to see that all those occasions where I'd pushed myself to the point of self-imposed anxiety, all those times where I'd criticised myself for 'getting things wrong' and allowed my mind to run away in rumination or judged myself harshly, I was actually not being very loving towards myself. During these times, I wasn't giving myself the compassion, support, and encouragement that I needed, despite it being something that I found so easy to give to other people in my life.

Being a do-it-all woman was admirable and I take nothing away from how I was, but it left little space for my own personal wants and needs. Wanting to take care of our loved ones is natural and doing our utmost to achieve that is by no means a bad thing, but it's all about striking the right balance and remembering to include ourselves in finding that balance. It took learning about self-love and self-care and starting its application to my own life for me to begin to learn to become my own best friend.

To be clear though, I have no regrets and I wouldn't change anything about my past, because I have been fortunate to have lived a very blessed and full life so far, brimful of wonderfully enriching experiences and deep connections. And wanting to do my best and be my best is still something that I value about myself even to this day. The way we live our lives and all the things we learn along the way moulds us into the person we are, and I am acutely aware that being my own tough taskmaster allowed me to develop a mental and physical toughness that has served me well.

Instead, in looking back and in knowing what I know now, I would wrap my younger self in a loving embrace, especially during those times of anguish and uncertainty, and reassure her that everything will be just fine and will work out for the highest good. We can still achieve the things we want to in life, even if we are kind, encouraging, supportive and gentle with ourselves. Loving-kindness is not weakness.

Better-qualified people have written at length about the power and importance of self-love, and I encourage you to read further should your interest be piqued. Here I offer my simple take on the subject, which is to say that, at its very core, self-love boils down to learning to become and then continuing to be our own best friend.

I'm not sure what it's like for youngsters these days, but a great many of us, especially of my generation and older (I am 48 years old at the time of writing), are really hard on ourselves. I think this is particularly true for a lot of us women who were brought up to be 'good girls' and carried a lot of guilt if we didn't conform. Even those of us who are wonderful to our friends and are bubbly and charming towards others have a tendency to talk to ourselves in ways that few people would tolerate. Before I learnt about self-love, my automatic response to myself when I made a mistake used to be, *Oh, you stupid woman*, or something along those lines, and I'd be really hard on myself about it for way longer than it warranted. I'm sure many people can relate to this.

Becoming our own best friend involves becoming mindful of our own negative self-talk and learning to notice when we're treating ourselves harshly, such as when we're self-judging or criticising, or when we don't offer ourselves patience and compassion. It means training ourselves to offer the grace and kindness that we would readily and easily give to our best friends back to us. To reiterate though, I'm not encouraging arrogance, vanity or egotism here, but self-compassion, patience and kindness.

For anyone new to this, I would definitely encourage you to educate yourself on the topic of self-love and learn to practise it. In the two or so years since I started doing this work, I have been able to transform my own self-talk from critical to supportive, from judgemental to encouraging, and I'm much gentler and kinder to myself than I used to be. Over this time I've nurtured a fondness for myself that equals that which I hold for my dearest friends, and I feel much more at ease with and at peace within myself as a consequence.

So as we find the pieces of our jigsaw puzzle and slot them into place and the picture builds up, whilst we might not be able to change the pieces already laid down, we are able to reflect on them and use them to shape our future puzzle pieces.

Self-love is also about taking time and making the effort to understand our own past emotional wounding acquired through our traumas, both big (like a divorce) and small (like not getting cuddles and kisses as children) and healing them, liberating us from the things that trigger us so that we can find inner peace and joy. As we become happier within ourselves, this allows us to be more present and conscious with others, and more loving.

The passage of time can be insufficient to heal emotional wounds. Time might lessen the intensity of the emotion, but left unattended, it can come back to bite us further down the line and if the wounding is significant (such as through trauma) or persistent enough, it can manifest into physical symptoms at a later date. When we break a bone, a doctor needs to attend to it to ensure that it is set and mends properly, otherwise it could heal in a non-optimal way or take unnecessarily long to do so.

The same applies when we suffer emotional injuries: we need to attend to them so they heal properly, through the application of inner healing work.

Even if you don't think you need to do this work, you have nothing to lose and everything to gain from learning about it and giving it a go. I had always been a generally happy and optimistic person even before doing this work, but practising it has brought an inner peace that was lacking previously and the small things that used to bother me a great deal have become insignificant.

To love ourselves is also to know ourselves and vice versa - it's robust self-acceptance. We deserve to take the time and make the effort to get to know our beings in a profoundly deep and honest way, through paying close attention to our thoughts, emotions and behaviours. And, most importantly, it's then having the courage to accept all parts of us, such as the jealous part, the controlling part, the insecure part, without judgement, whether we like them or not, just as we do with our best friends, who we accept and love regardless of their foibles.

It's also having compassion for ourselves when we discover those sides of us that we might not have been aware of before and which we deem less desirable, knowing that they are most likely a result of our life conditioning. And it is the recognition that we personally have the ability to change anything that doesn't serve us or the greater good - the power is in our hands.

By way of an example, when I was little, I had a couple of experiences where girls who I considered to be friends treated me unkindly, causing me to acquire a mild mistrust of women growing up. And whilst I did have a lot of female friends at university and in my twenties and thirties, and despite my closest friends being female, I generally preferred the company of men socially. I found them more straightforward, less judgemental and more fun to hang out with, and I felt more comfortable with them.

I've always been a bit of a tomboy, preferring pursuits that were more male-dominated in my day (snowboarding, surfing, climbing), so I was happy just hanging out with the guys and having a laugh. I didn't really think much of it, it was just the way I was. But as I started to do my inner work, I realised that there was a subtle child-like insecurity within me around being friends with women, barring a few notable exceptions.[3]

As adults, we don't like to think of ourselves as having insecurities because it makes us seem weak or flawed, but befriending ourselves creates space for us to acknowledge these sides to us with compassion and kindness. So I used what I'd learnt and applied some techniques to heal this part of me, and it's been truly liberating and empowering.

Something else we don't usually think about as adults is having to make new friends; it sort of takes us back to being at school. But after my divorce, having been a mother and a wife for so long, I actively sought out opportunities to meet new people, to widen my network and invest in new friendships as something for me. In the past year, I've cultivated new deep and trusting friendships with a few wonderful women who I'm mightily fond of and can be totally myself with. And I no longer feel any unease meeting new women or being in their company, and I'm now as comfortable with them as I have always been with men. And if you go into an activity such as meeting new people with an open mind, a curious mindset and a spirit of adventure, it's a lot of fun! Everyone we meet has something interesting for us to learn from if we are open and receptive.

---

[3] I have been fortunate enough to have a few wonderful female friends who were my rocks when I split up with my husband, to whom I'm truly grateful.

Another reason to become our own best friend is that only we know how we truly feel in any given moment, and as much as we might be loved by others around us, there will be times when we are our only company and our sole counsel in moments of challenge. Becoming our own best friend allows us to know love and to feel loved on the inside without the need for people, things or events occurring on the outside: it means not feeling lonely even when we're alone. In this way, becoming our own best friend enables us to develop our own inner confidence from which we can generate inner love and joy whenever we want and wherever we find ourselves in life.

And as social creatures, there's no doubt that we need other people, and they can and do bring us tremendous love, joy, support and comfort. But if we entrust all of our happiness and sense of self-worth to external factors, be that people or possessions, not only are we more heavily impacted when those things are gone, even if only for a short while, but we also do ourselves a great disservice in depriving ourselves of the gift of realising our own intrinsic value.

When we know our own worth, we can gain liberation from our own self-imposed emotional and mental shackles caused by attachment to external things and people. That's not to say that we should hold any part of ourselves back in our relationships (of all types), for deep connection with others is what bonds us and creates richness in our lives, but simply that we learn to appreciate our own inherent worthiness independent of externalities.

In the early days after splitting from my now ex-husband, the time after putting my boys to bed brought such intense loneliness - it had been many, many years since I'd been alone in the evenings. But the deeper into my inner work I went, the stronger the connection with myself grew and the more I opened my heart to self-love, the more the sense of loneliness abated until it extinguished altogether. And it wasn't long before I was very happily spending whole days on my own when the boys were with their dad without feeling lonely in the slightest.

When we're accustomed to being with and around other people, being by ourselves takes some getting used to, but that's all it is - conditioning - and thus not something to fear. And that's not to say that I prefer my own company to that of my loved ones, simply that I am equally happy with both. And as we adapt to being comfortable being on our own, we become happier within ourselves, which, in turn, translates to us being happier people for our loved ones to be with. Learning to be happy on my own allowed me to focus on and be present with my boys when they were with me.

And as we cement our trust and love of ourselves, we establish strong and defined sides to our jigsaw puzzle; edges and boundaries that we can be sure about and rely on, helping us to be grounded in our lives and within ourselves.

Becoming our own best friend also involves becoming aware of and tending to our own needs. As parents and spouses, we can sometimes unwittingly sacrifice our own well-being for the happiness of our families, thinking that this is the right thing to do. Towards the end of my marriage, I'd been a mother and a wife for so long that I kind of felt like I'd lost my own sense of identity. And whilst the break-up was undoubtedly deeply painful, it did bring liberation in some ways because I gained time, when the boys were with their dad, to focus on myself. Sometimes when we're in the midst of the hecticness of our roles as parents/partners/carers, running around helping and sorting everyone else out, we forget that taking time for ourselves allows us to replenish our own cups so that we have the capacity to tend to our loved ones better.

But tending to our own needs also means learning to correctly identify what those needs should be. It's not necessarily about taking time to have bubble baths and facials, although these things can be of benefit for some people. It's about understanding ourselves and the effects that our thoughts and actions have on us. For instance, if engaging with social media leaves you in a negative mindset or contracted emotional state, reducing/minimising exposure can help. Or if you are already feeling stressed out due to having too much on your plate and someone asks you to help them with something, it's okay to politely decline, even if you find it difficult because of a sense of obligation. Tending to our own needs includes setting personal boundaries in order to manage our stress levels.

As already explained, it's no bad thing to want to do and be our best but it can sometimes work against us if taken to the extreme and we don't take care of ourselves. When we learn to love ourselves, we cut ourselves some slack when we mess up, we learn to show ourselves compassion and be our own counsel when we have uncomfortable emotions and we learn to make choices that are in our own best interests, not just that of others. By becoming our own best friend, we learn to do and be our best in a way that is both of service to others and also loving and supportive of ourselves.

And finally, in my opinion, self-love is about being comfortable acknowledging our own strengths and uniqueness. Growing up, to blow one's own trumpet was seen as bragging or boasting. Like many Asians of my generation or older, I was brought up to be self-effacing, modest and humble. And whilst I agree that these traits are more serving than arrogance and egotism, it does render one uncomfortable when appreciating and openly expressing one's qualities for fear of being seen to be pretentious, vain or arrogant.

My family and I came to the UK as Vietnamese refugees (we're Chinese but were born in Vietnam). Those who were alive and can remember the 1970s may recall *the Boat People*, people who fled Vietnam in wooden boats under treacherous conditions, often unsure of their final destination, simply seeking safer shores. Many lost their lives during those times, entire boats crammed with people fleeing oppression and hoping for freedom eradicated by the rage of violent seas.

The wooden boat we were in was burdened with over double the boat's capacity of passengers, with very little food and water and woefully inadequate sanitation. One of my sisters nearly fatally suffocated from lack of oxygen below deck where we were stowed. Another sister saw the body of a baby that had died thrown overboard, not out of heartlessness but of sheer necessity. As I write this, I am startled to find myself crying for the grief of the baby's parents.

By the goodness of grace, our little boat was rescued by a British ship and we were eventually brought safely to the UK, albeit with virtually just the shirts on our backs, having both sacrificed and lost all of our worldly possessions in search of freedom. With no money and only the clothes we were wearing to our names, we relied on the charity and generosity of the British government and public to provide us with our basic needs, for which we were truly grateful. Through my parents' resilience and strong work ethic, working every hour God sent, and their ability to economise, spending any money we had as wisely and frugally as possible, in time we were able to forge a simple but comfortable life for ourselves.

This start in life profoundly coloured my life perspective and gave me an appreciation for the little things, like a roof over my head and food in my belly. It also gifted me with tenacity, resilience and fortitude. Before I learnt about self-love, I was pretty nonchalant about this chapter of my life, always regarding it as no big deal. But since embarking on my self-love journey, I've come to develop a deep appreciation and reverence for what my family and I endured and the role it played in shaping me, and I now no longer have any qualms about expressing this openly and proudly.

My story doesn't make me special. There are millions of people around the world with similar stories to mine. None of us is more or less special than anyone else. But equally, we are each and every one of us special in our own uniqueness. There will only ever be one of me, with my unique view of the world based on my unique personality and life experience, just like there will only ever be one of you, with yours. And the more we individually and collectively embrace our own and others' uniqueness, the more we realise that whilst we are all different, we are all connected through our collective humanity. Acceptance of our fellow humans living on this planet of ours helps us to become more compassionate towards each other. And thus self-love becomes love generally and universally.

Everyone has their own story of adversity and challenge, but living through significant traumatic events isn't necessary to build up courage and fortitude. We can foster it if we have love for ourselves, through believing and knowing that we have agency for our own happiness, and through knowing that we have the capacity to endure and overcome life's challenges; that we can choose how we want that completed puzzle picture to look.

It's worth noting that cultivating self-love doesn't mean downgrading or even relinquishing our responsibilities in our roles as parents, partners, friends and so forth. It's simply the recognition that by taking better care of ourselves, we can show up more fully in all areas of our lives and serve others in a way that is loving to ourselves. This allows us to have the capacity to appreciate our role in the greater collective. When we understand that we are part of something bigger than ourselves, self-love enables us to recognise the importance of our individual contribution towards the greater good.

Through working on my own self-love, I built up the courage to write this book. Prior to doing my inner work, despite my own adventurous and outgoing nature, I would have had way too many inhibitions and insecurities to have created it. I would have been too worried about what people would think of it, about whether anyone would bother reading it, worried about people's judgement. But when we know our own self-worth and love who we are, we become less worried about not being liked, or not getting other people's approval.

And we can do what we feel is right if that's what we want on our puzzle picture, even if it scares us. We can write a book, not for ourselves or what it can bring for us, but for others to read because we believe that our story can help someone else out there. When we believe in something bigger than and beyond ourselves, our fears, whilst they might not disappear entirely, no longer remain an obstacle.

So I urge anyone out there who has been able to relate to any of what I've shared and doesn't know about self-love, or feels like they could be more loving towards themselves, to learn about it and the different ways in which you can love yourself more. Most of them are really simple and don't require any special skill or knowledge, such as the process of noticing our negative self-talk and changing it to be more positive and empowering.

But simple doesn't necessarily equate to easy. Changing our negative self-talk is a very simple alteration that can be made, but that doesn't make it easy if we've been self-judging and criticising all our lives. We have to remember that we're trying to change decades of habits and accept that it will take some time, and be self-compassionate if it takes a while to get the hang of it.

For me personally, after decades of mental and emotional toughness, self-love didn't come naturally and required, and still requires, conscious effort and a commitment and dedication to making it a daily practice.

At the heart of it, self-love is a commitment to our own personal growth, changing our own perception of who we are and our attitude towards us for the better. It's a commitment to know and understand ourselves in a deeply profound way and to support becoming our most authentic, joyful, liberated and highest version in our lifetimes. We invest so much time and energy in external people and things, some of which bring us questionable benefit. Yet we devote relatively little time to the one person who is the most important in our lives, namely ourselves, and self-love is the recognition of this - the becoming of our own best friend. It's no coincidence that the longest chapter of this book is on this, *Personal Growth and Evolution*.

We have nothing to lose and everything to gain in embarking on this important quest of nurturing our own self-love. When we work towards a better, more loving (compassionate, kinder, patient and so forth) and happier version of ourselves, we become better in all our roles: better parents, better partners, better friends and colleagues. And thus we are able to bring more joy into our own little worlds through the ripple effects of our love. And if enough of us take on this mantle to create a critical mass, that joy will ripple out to the world at large.

And so it is, we contribute to a more loving and more glorious version of not only our own completed jigsaw puzzle picture but also the collective universal one as well.

CHAPTER 3

FORGIVENESS

Prior to splitting up with my now ex-husband, I held the core belief that if he were to cheat on me, I would never be able to forgive him. It was something that I believed so vehemently that there was no room for doubt, no room for wondering 'what if?', on a par with knowing that my eyes are brown.

Then came the day when I found out that my husband was having an affair. And not just a fling or a short-lived thing, but a proper full-blown affair where he had been living a double life for an extended period of time. As clichéd as it sounds, it did actually feel like the world as I knew it was unequivocally crashing down.

For some, an affair doesn't necessarily spell the end of a marriage, but for me personally, it did. There was no going back from the betrayal and demolition of trust of this proportion. Discovering that I'd been lied to and deceived by the person I thought I trusted the most brought seismic pain and trauma. And then to make matters worse, three weeks after the fateful day of discovery, COVID Lockdown 1.0 was implemented in the UK. To say that it was a low point in my life is somewhat of an understatement. You could make a movie out of the whole thing, how it happened, how I found out and the resulting aftermath - it would be quite a drama indeed!

But that's not for here. This chapter is about forgiveness.

As you can imagine, anger was the dominant emotion that featured at the time, along with hurt and utter disbelief. I felt a rage that I had never imagined possible for me to feel. It pervaded my thoughts and brought about countless sleepless nights. The whole experience was immensely traumatic and in those first few weeks, I felt consumed by my own thoughts and emotions. Looking back, it's a wonder that I was still able to function normally, but I managed to find the wherewithal to continue working and caring for my children as usual. And I consider myself incredibly blessed with the fortitude that enabled me to shield my children from what was happening within me and between me and my ex-husband.

But after several weeks of being angry, I realised that not only was it not serving me, but that it was also starting to seriously affect my emotional and mental state. I couldn't think straight, I wasn't eating properly and I wasn't sleeping. And I guess I just reached the point of surrender, where I thought, *Right, that's it. I've had enough of feeling like this, I'm not doing this anymore.*

When you see the futility and harm of staying in a certain state, you are able to think with more clarity. It was at that point that I decided resolutely and made a commitment to myself that I was not going to let the affair define me. I knew that I got to choose how I wanted to interpret what happened and how I would be affected by it. And that meant letting go of the anger first.

And actually, if I'm totally honest, given the strong views I had on infidelity, deciding to let go of the anger was easier than I thought it would be. I'm not saying that the actual act of letting go of it was easy; it has felt nigh on impossible at times and I've had to dig deep to find the inner strength, but making the decision was easy. And once the decision was made, blessed relief followed promptly. I felt so much lighter, as if a huge boulder had been lifted off my chest.

I've always been resilient and strong-willed. Whether this is a virtue of my own personality or a consequence of my seemingly challenging start in life (which I explained in the previous chapter), it's hard to say. I suspect it's a combination of the two. Either way, I feel blessed to have had this to fall back on at this juncture because it equipped me with the tenacity to not be a victim of my circumstances, giving me the conviction and resolve to forge my own path of healing.

It allowed me to keep a level head despite my internal turmoil. My children were innocent in all of this and it was paramount that they shouldn't suffer because of it. I was adamant that I would ensure that the impact on them of us splitting up would be as minimal as was in my power.

My love for my children and my sense of responsibility for them made forgiveness an easy decision. My ex would always be their dad and I wasn't going to deprive them of that. And, as such, he would always be in their lives, and hence consequently always in mine. If I wanted them to be happy, then we needed to be as amicable as we could feasibly be: we needed to find a way to be the best co-parents that we could be. Our boys needed to know that despite us splitting up, they would still have a loving family. It might look a little different but they would still be loved by both of us, no matter what.

When we take a wide-angled view and see the bigger picture, it changes our perspective on things. Focussing on what had happened and succumbing to a victimhood mentality would have kept me stuck in the mire of misery, but if I wanted to achieve the highest possible outcome from this situation, namely our children's happiness as well as my own, forgiveness was the only option.

In keeping our jigsaw puzzles in our awareness, especially during challenging times, we are reminded to zoom out and see that bigger picture. And in doing so, we are assisted in making more empowered decisions and in taking more loving actions.

I've always been fascinated by the human psyche and have enjoyed reading articles on human behaviour and personal development over the years. By this point, I had already long been aware of the concept that events affect us based on our interpretations of them. In the same way that two people can look at the same picture and see it very differently based on how they're feeling, we can view events in our lives differently based on our perspectives. It's the lens through which we choose to view things that colours our experience of them.

So I knew that if I took the viewpoint that my husband had cheated on me, my mindset would be that he had perpetrated wrongdoing against me, automatically rendering me a victim of his actions and thus subject to the corresponding thought patterns of *how could he do that to me* and *what an evil so-and-so*.

However, if I were to adopt the perspective that he simply had an affair, his infidelity became simply something that he had done, removing the personal element of it being something he had done to me. And whilst that's not to say I was unaffected (I was deeply so), taking this perspective permitted a level of objectivity and rationality which made coping with my emotions more bearable. And it ultimately empowered me to overcome the worst of it much more quickly than if I'd allowed myself to stay stuck in victimhood.

I should point out here that I am no superhero, I did succumb to these thought patterns initially, in the early days when the wound was still raw - I am human after all. But it was relatively short-lived and I didn't stay on those thought trains for very long as I knew that they didn't serve me or anyone else.

As with the decision to let go of anger, the decision to forgive was the easy part. The actual implementation was most definitely not and seemed at times insurmountably harder than letting go of the anger. Periodically, emotions would arise that would trigger a fervent desire for my ex-husband to understand how I felt and suffer similar emotional pain, but causing misery to others, whilst it might feel gratifying in the moment, benefits nobody in the long run. Our boys needed both parents to be present and loving amidst the chaos and turmoil of separation, coupled with the impact of COVID.

One thing to note though, is that forgiving is not the same as forgetting. Forgiving someone doesn't mean you condone their actions or overlook them, but simply that you no longer bear them malice for what they did. Much has been written about the power of forgiveness and the benefits it brings, and I encourage anyone who isn't already aware of this to educate themselves on it if curiosity beckons.

From my own personal experience of making the decision to forgive, I know that my life is infinitely better because I did. My children are significantly happier than they would have been had I held onto the anger and permitted it to dictate my behaviour by treating my ex with hostility and animosity.

It enabled us to keep the suffering to a minimum and to cultivate, over time, an incredibly amicable relationship as co-parents that serves our children's highest good. It has also enabled us to spend time together as a foursome and to provide a level of continuity and stability for our children that wouldn't have been achievable otherwise. A significant milestone that pays testament to how far we've come was marked in December 2022 when we went on our first family skiing holiday together.

Forgiveness has allowed me to see that my ex-husband isn't a bad man, despite his past behaviour. In fact, he has many redeeming qualities and is actually a decent guy who is there for me and our boys when we need him. And whilst he might be a 'weekend dad', he does take his parenting responsibilities seriously. He just lost his way and made some terrible decisions based on his level of consciousness at the time. Sure, he still has his issues that he needs to work on, as do I. And we still have the odd argument here and there, which is to be expected. To judge him serves nobody and a more helpful course of action, for both me and our children, is to support him in his growth through acceptance and appreciation of who he is, warts and all.

That said, I fully appreciate that an amicable relationship like the one my ex and I have cultivated is not always possible or even desired, where the wounds are too deep and the hurt caused is too painful to overcome. This is especially true where the party who committed adultery is not willing to acknowledge the pain that they have caused. I consider myself lucky that despite everything, at least my ex was remorseful once he'd realised the impact of his actions, as I understand that this is not always the case. So in telling my story, I'm not suggesting by any means that my path is right for anyone else, simply that this is what worked for me and to provide an example of what is possible if the circumstances allow. We can't control how the other person behaves and so we can only focus on ourselves in aiming for the highest outcome within our power.

Most importantly of all, for me personally, forgiveness empowered me to start the healing process and find inner peace much more rapidly than I would have done had I chosen to re-side in the comfort of self-pity and victimhood. Succumbing to our emotions when we feel that someone has wronged us is basic human nature and can feel good in the moment, so we must have self-compassion if we find ourselves there. But to stay in that space for longer than necessary only leads to our own suffering, where we become victims of, and trapped by, our own emotions. Forgiveness facilitates our own emotional liberation.

Having said that though, for true forgiveness to take place, emotional readiness is necessary. I was only ready to forgive once I'd been able to process the initial grief and anger sufficiently for the wound to be less raw. And this bit is crucially important; you need to be ready in order to be able to truly forgive. It's not something we or anyone else can force us into. It's not enough to simply know intellectually that forgiveness is the best course of action. You need to get yourself to the point where emotionally, you feel it too. And understanding what you can achieve through the act of forgiveness can get you there faster.

Sometimes, it's not until we are faced with challenges that we know what strengths we possess. Had it not been for the affair, I wouldn't have known my own capacity for forgiveness, my resilience, tenacity and fortitude. And I say this not to blow my own trumpet, but to point out that through adversity, we come to know ourselves. And in knowing ourselves, we build up our own inner confidence; confidence in our capacity to not only endure but to thrive, giving us the courage to become better versions of ourselves. And in doing so, we make better, more conscious choices not just for ourselves, but for others around us.

It's worth noting here that forgiveness isn't necessarily a one-and-done thing, especially if the hurt was very deep. In the time since I decided to forgive my ex-husband, as we are still very much in each other's lives, there have been occasions where anger has come up for me, triggered by a niggle that hadn't yet been healed. During these instances, I still accepted and honoured my emotions, but each time, I made a conscious decision to forgive and it helped me to move past my anger and hurt in that moment. And now I'm happy to say that the occasional disagreements we have are mostly (but not always) just the standard ones that most parents have when bringing up children, rather than being related to my emotional state around the affair.

When considering whether to write this chapter of the book, I was initially concerned about having an adverse effect on our children, given that my ex and I hadn't told them what actually happened when we split up. We had simply said that we had stopped loving each other and were arguing frequently and so had made the difficult decision to part ways. Also, I didn't want to negatively influence my boys' impression of their dad and undermine the relationship he has with them. After all, this was the original rationale for telling them what we did in the first place.

But after over three years of role modelling that parents splitting up doesn't need to be a bad thing and that we can still have a loving family dynamic, albeit a somewhat unconventional one, I am now confident that knowing the truth will actually help us to convey to our boys how much they are loved. They will know that our love for them gave rise to our prioritising their well-being and happiness ahead of our own issues, shielding them from any potential harm it could have caused. It also clearly demonstrates that it is perfectly possible to transcend life's challenges and undesired events, given the appropriate motivation. In this instance, that motivation was our love for them.[4]

And as we make more empowered and loving decisions in our lives, guided by a desire for a greater good that transcends our own challenges, we contribute to a more stunning version of our own jigsaw puzzle pictures.

In addition to the forgiveness of others, the other side of forgiveness is forgiveness for ourselves. My amazing parents always taught us good values and morals, which included being respectful and kind towards others, so I've always tried to be a good and decent person who is considerate of others. But once I started my inner work, I reflected back on my life and identified times when I'd behaved in ways that could have been more loving to people close to me. I could have been kinder with my words or less flippant with my actions, and whilst I know I was never intentionally unkind during those occasions, the outcome was that I inadvertently hurt the feelings of the people involved without meaning to. Inner work makes you more aware, more conscious of your thoughts and emotions, your words and your actions, enabling you to choose a higher course of action.

Initially, as I raised my own levels of consciousness, I found myself wracked with guilt over those times, even though I know that it's just water under the bridge now for those involved. But as I started doing more work on self-love, I understood that to hold onto the guilt didn't serve me or anyone else. I learnt that the more loving thing to do was to forgive myself, which I did, after atoning through apologising to those that I needed to.

---

[4] My ex and I knew that our boys would eventually find out what really happened sooner or later, and so decided that it was better that the truth comes from us, explained in as loving a way as possible so that they could understand it from our perspective rather than through other means. Prior to publication, we sat down as a family and discussed this in a way that allows for the highest good.

Forgiving ourselves for our mistakes doesn't mean we don't take accountability for our words and actions; we still do that, especially when we've adversely affected someone else, even if it's inadvertently or unintentionally. But we use those mistakes as opportunities to learn and grow, and we forgive ourselves afterwards, rather than beating ourselves up about them. And thus, forgiveness, of ourselves as well as others, brings healing and benefits for all parties and whilst it might not be easy to do, it is definitely worth the effort.

So in summary, forgiveness is ultimately an act of both love and self-love. To forgive oneself is simply self-love. To forgive another might, on the face of it, seem like an act of love towards the other person, but by releasing ourselves from the shackles of our own harmful thoughts and emotions, we see that, fundamentally, the forgiveness of others is also an act of self-love.

And as we grow our own personal forgiveness muscle, the easier it becomes to forgive, to the point where it becomes easier to not get or stay angry at people when we think they've wronged us. But it's not something that necessarily comes easily, and it requires persistent practice and patience, as well as compassion and self-forgiveness when we get it wrong.

And as with the previous chapters, if we keep relating this back to our jigsaw puzzles, as we learn to forgive ourselves and others, we are able to craft our pictures more beautifully, more kindly and, ultimately, more lovingly.

CHAPTER 4

HEALING, SELF-CARE AND PRACTICE

Growing up in a household with four children and busy, hard-working parents meant that my siblings and I became self-sufficient at an early age. So I've always preferred to at least try to do things for myself where I can, before seeking help from others if I reach the point where it's necessary.

And thus, after discovering my ex's affair and suffering the initial turmoil, it wasn't long before I started to seek out information on how to support myself in dealing with and managing my emotions. Throughout my life, I have always been interested in physical fitness and nutrition, so I have always exercised regularly, eaten reasonably healthily and tried to get sufficient sleep. But I knew relatively little about mental and emotional health, so I had a lot of learning to do.

And thank goodness for the internet! For all the modern problems that it and social media have given rise to, there's no doubt that the internet can be a source of tremendous benefit if used wisely. Apart from the vital support and comfort I derived from speaking with family and friends (and I can't stress enough how critical this was), everything I used to help me on my healing journey was found on the internet.

One of the most significant things that I learnt was the importance of processing our emotions. It's imperative that we process strong emotions from traumatic events and heal from them, otherwise they can stay stuck in our emotional bodies where they can potentially manifest into either physical or emotional symptoms further down the line.

Growing up, having big emotions was discouraged and certainly processing them was not something we were ever taught, either at home or at school. This is by no means a criticism of my schooling, or my parents who are unequivocally wonderfully kind, caring, gentle, wise and selfless people who sacrificed everything they had in the hope of providing a better future for our family.

My parents brought us up in the best way they knew how and have taught us a great many things, which included instilling good morals and values in us and most importantly, role-modelling how to be comprehensively decent human beings. But they themselves were unaware of the importance of processing emotions or how to go about it when we were growing up, and so I had to learn this for myself as an adult.

And I was a diligent student, fuelled by a passion that erupted from the heart, borne out of a desire to find inner peace, and needed no encouragement. I devoured content like the hungry caterpillar, learning from a vast and diverse set of mentors who have generously given away their knowledge freely online, in service of their fellow humans.

I armed myself with information, listening to podcast after podcast and talks on the internet whilst I did the housework or exercised at home in the mornings. Any spare minute when I didn't have my sons was dedicated to educating myself, and such was my eagerness to learn that it never felt like effort.

And from my learning, one of the most powerful things I did for myself was to make space to cry. I'd never been someone who cried much up until then, always keeping my emotions in check, subconsciously seeing it as a sign of weakness. Plus, initially, anger and pride prevented me from even acknowledging that I was feeling any sadness; *I don't need him, I'll be perfectly fine on my own,* I told myself. But a part of me knew that I was just being childishly defensive and, despite the prevalence of that anger and pride, when I thought about it rationally, I realised that in spite of the affair, I possessed a cavernous and overwhelming sadness at the loss of my marriage and the break-up of our family unit.

So, after learning about the stages of grief and the importance of processing the emotions of grief appropriately and adequately, one day when I found myself alone, I consciously and intentionally let down my guard and surrendered to my sorrow, making way for the emotions within me to pour forth without restraint, and simply allowed myself to cry. Before long, I was sobbing great torrents of tears as I'd never done before, experiencing a part of me previously unknown to myself. In permitting myself to be vulnerable and in making space for my grief, I opened the floodgates and I cried and cried, then cried some more, until it felt like all my tears had run dry. And I was elated to discover that it was hugely cathartic, bringing a blessed reprieve and release from the intensity of emotions swirling around inside me.

It's sort of funny because, having never been someone who cried very much, after my first massive sobbing session I remember laughing out loud to myself, feeling like some crazy woman who had lost her senses. But I understood the necessity of it and felt completely at ease with it afterwards. And whilst it certainly wasn't the final time I cried with regards to the end of my marriage, its impact was poignant, deeply felt and marked an important turning point for me in how I process my emotions. No longer do I deny my uncomfortable feelings, or push them aside. I acknowledge and embrace them instead, accepting that they are a part of me that need to be expressed, and then I lovingly release them.

Even if you think that crying wouldn't be your chosen or preferred way for processing painful emotions like sadness and grief, the salient point here is not the method deployed, but the fact that they get processed.

I think many in my generation and older were brought up to keep our emotions in check, to keep a stiff upper lip, but in doing so, we never learnt to truly feel those emotions, depriving us of the opportunity to acquire the skills to manage them.

When we allow ourselves to witness, feel, identify and label our uncomfortable emotions and become aware of the thoughts and feelings that they invoke within us rather than denying them, two things can happen. Firstly, we can build up a tolerance for uncomfortable emotions because we know we've endured and survived them before and thus can do so again, thereby rendering them less scary because we recognise our capacity for having difficult feelings. And secondly, we can seek to understand the feelings within us that those emotions evoke, enabling us to reframe them more helpfully so that we can experience them more positively. I write more on this latter point in the *Personal Growth and Evolution* chapter.

But emotions need to be managed productively and whilst they shouldn't be suppressed, that's not to say they always need to be expressed outwardly towards others either. In some cases, they just need to be acknowledged and released.

There's a difference in learning how to manage emotions in the moment and in the long term. If you're angry with someone at a given moment, you don't need to shout at them to release that anger (even though that's precisely what you might feel like doing); other more loving ways can be found to do so, such as adopting certain breathing techniques to calm down your nervous system right there and then. But if that anger is protracted, it might be more helpful to take up practices such as meditation to manage your stress levels in general. Additionally, understanding the root cause of that anger can help you learn to reframe your perspective and thus avoid getting triggered in the first place.

And it's the releasing of those painful or less desirable emotions that's vital for our own mental and emotional well-being. Different techniques might be more effective for releasing different emotions. As explained, sadness can be released through crying, and protracted anger towards a person can be released through forgiveness meditations, for instance.

I continued to build up my knowledge, learning about psychology, neuroscience and different types of psychotherapy and modalities for managing our emotions. Most importantly, I learnt how all the parts of us that are both visible and invisible, tangible and intangible, are intrinsically connected and how healing and self-care needs to incorporate all those different areas (our bodies, minds and emotions) for us to thrive. It's futile to maintain the windows of a house whilst allowing the roof to fall into disrepair if we want that house to last a long time, and it's the same for our bodies - we have to take care of ourselves holistically for optimal health.

And as we learn to do this, caring for all parts of us (mind, body and spirit) collectively, rather than as separate entities, we build up our jigsaw puzzles in a more rounded manner, being able to fill in sections at a time rather than little disparate parts here and there.

In the same way that most of us know that we need to eat well, sleep well and exercise to maintain our physical health, if we neglect our mental and emotional health, our physical bodies will suffer, maybe not immediately, but eventually. And as already mentioned, unprocessed emotional wounds can eventually present themselves as physical or mental ailments. Many of the talks that I listened to recounted examples where patients with long-term medical conditions saw them subside or disappear after they worked on their emotional stressors.

This book focuses predominantly on mental and emotional health, mainly because that's where my growth has been and led to the writing of it, and because physical health and fitness is already well documented. But as I've said, you can't have one and not the other. So everything in this book rests upon an underlying assumption that the body is already being cared for, through regular exercise, sufficient quality sleep and a healthy diet that suits the individual.

Everything that I was learning was immensely fascinating and absorbing, with one teaching leading onto another and then another. Every talk I listened to would reveal at least one new gem of insight, or a new area for me to explore and excavate. But the ardent accumulation of information can only get us so far. You can't think your way to healing: you need to practise and embody your learning.

It's of little use learning about the importance of meditation or the effectiveness of breathing techniques if nothing is done about it. I took on the challenge of adopting and putting my learning into practice with enthusiasm and rigour, such was my desire for inner peace. I experimented with some of the techniques that I learnt to calm my nerves (such as tapping/emotional freedom technique and certain breathing techniques)[5] whenever I found

---

[5] See appendix for more information.

myself getting stressed or panicked, to see which I found most effective. And I started to meditate daily, again trialling different types to find the ones that suited me or that resonated with me.

It's worth noting here that even though I started meditating, this was only really helpful in conjunction with the more important task of learning to regulate my nervous system to begin with. The trauma of finding out about the affair left my nervous system so dysregulated that for the first couple of months afterwards, small stressors would have a huge impact on me, and I would be left feeling like my heart was pounding so loudly as to be audible, or like the blood was draining from my body. But I was a woman on a mission and fervently learnt about the nervous system and how to regulate it, and I practised it; it was this that enabled me to carry on with my day-to-day life amidst the tumult and barrage of my emotions.

There are many techniques out there and I outline the main ones I found helpful in the appendix, but everyone's traumas and how they are affected by them differ, and techniques that work for one person may well be ineffectual for another. Therefore, rather than making recommendations, it's more helpful for me to encourage anyone in need of help regulating their nervous system to seek out information and ascertain which methods their own mind and body respond well to. Thankfully we are in an era where the importance of mental and emotional health is widely recognised and so a quick internet search returns an abundance of information.

Also, whilst much has been written about the benefits of meditation and I personally found it helpful, it's important to point out that it's not necessarily right for everyone, especially if trauma has been experienced and the nervous system is dysregulated. For some, it can be counterproductive if nervous system regulation hasn't been established beforehand, as attempting to meditate could actually create further stress if they believe it's not being done correctly, for example. Once again, it's imperative that each person undertakes to understand their own needs and tends to them accordingly.

Each person's jigsaw puzzle is as unique as their individual set of fingerprints, and so is the combination of modalities and techniques for healing and self-care that will work optimally for them.

Another thing that's worth noting is the importance of taking care of our bodies and minds when times are good and life is ticking along nicely so that we are more prepared if, and when, unexpected events strike. Thanks to my upbringing (my dad has always exercised every day and my mum cooked us healthy food) as well as my own interest in health and fitness, I have always been pretty healthy, exercising regularly, eating reasonably well and sleeping as well as can be expected with young children. And whilst I'm not saying that anything really could have prepared me for finding out about the affair, with hindsight, I know that having this foundation of a healthy body and mind through decades of self-care meant that my own trauma didn't hit me anywhere near as hard as it would have otherwise done.

When we take care of all parts of us (mind, body and spirit), whilst it doesn't make us impervious to life's inevitable challenges, it certainly helps us face them with more ease and grace than we otherwise would. And like we do with physical self-care (we exercise so that our bodies stay strong and we keep our teeth clean so that they will last as long as possible), making emotional self-care a daily habit will help us stay on an even keel and less subject to the ups and downs of life.

My healing journey relating to the affair wasn't plain sailing; I naturally had good days and bad days, and it took discipline over a period of time but eventually, I was able to arrive at a point where my emotions from the trauma of discovering the affair no longer had a stranglehold on me, and I felt strong and optimistic about what lay ahead.

What started off as a quest to heal my heart turned into a journey to heal other parts of me that I didn't even know needed healing. I learnt how our childhood and younger years play a vital role in shaping who we are, including our limiting beliefs and insecurities. I had actually read about this earlier on in my life but had always just thought it didn't apply to me.

I regarded myself as a well-rounded individual with a normal and non-traumatic upbringing. I'd worked hard and excelled at school and university, and had an interesting and varied career with a highly respected company that I'd been with for over twenty-three years since graduating. I'd been blessed with the opportunity to go on many adventures over my forty-five years of life at that point, having travelled extensively and taken up many activities which brought me fun and joy. My life so far had been pretty great and I had so much to be grateful for, so what was there to complain about?

I've already explained how incredible my parents are, so the idea that I needed to heal parts of me that had been affected by aspects of my upbringing and early life implied that there was something wrong with the way I'd been brought up. This, in turn, ignited a resistance in me that to even consider those things felt like a harsh and unjustified betrayal of my parents and everything that they'd sacrificed and done for us.

But in learning that we can still be impacted by things that happened to us as children and youngsters, whether that be at home, school or anywhere else, even by well-intentioned people, I was able to separate what needed healing within me from the people and events that took place which inadvertently caused them. This allowed me to heal those parts of me without blaming anyone or anything.

So to give you an example, when I was little, it was uncommon in Chinese families for parents to show affection to their children through hugs and kisses. This might sound a bit shocking and callous in this day and age in Western society, but this was normal in many Chinese families back then. The importance of hugs, kisses and words of affirmation for young children was not known about and the lack of these things was not intentional neglect or child cruelty. Therefore, as children, my siblings and I were rarely, if ever, hugged, kissed or told we were loved. This is simply a statement of how things were, with no blame, judgement or criticism of my beloved parents.

I love and appreciate my parents deeply and sincerely and have a profound respect for them, and I know they love us dearly too, but they brought us up in the way that they were brought up themselves. Their way of expressing their love for us as children was in providing for us, my dad through hard graft to earn money to feed and clothe us, my mum through cooking and cleaning for us, in addition to working herself. And for that, there is absolutely no room for questioning their selflessness, kindness and generosity. And I can't say that I didn't feel loved as a child, it was just different to the more affectionate way we care for children nowadays.

But when I started learning about how things in our childhood affect us as adults, I began to understand how this could have contributed to certain traits I had as an adult, such as a craving for affection and emotional closeness within relationships, yet not wanting to show neediness, for fear of appearing weak. And in knowing this about myself, I am empowered to create pieces of my own jigsaw puzzle that align to a higher version of the completed puzzle.

Prior to the affair, I confess to a level of arrogance that had me thinking that if someone needed to do inner work, it implied there was something wrong with them. But I learnt that this is far from the case and that it takes courage, humility and being honest with ourselves to recognise and acknowledge that there are parts of us that need healing.

And healing isn't necessarily a one-off thing like a magic bullet which eradicates our pain, we do a few meditations and healing practices and declare ourselves to be fully healed forever. Sometimes things that we think we've healed can still surface again if the wound was particularly deep, and it might take a few attempts or experimentation with different techniques to get it right.

People generally don't stick with things just because someone has told them to do it. They need to want to do it for themselves and have a strong enough 'why' as well as to be ready, willing and have the internal capacity. Thus, it is not for me to tell anyone to follow my healing journey, but in sharing what's possible through my own experience, my hope is to provide anyone in a similar situation with the impetus to begin their own journey once they feel ready.

But that's not to say I have it all figured out though. I've made mistakes in my life just like everybody else and will no doubt continue to do so. And as much as I will always endeavour to live a loving life, I'm certainly not immune to losing my cool with others, usually those closest to me. I am a perimenopausal, sometimes hormonal, single mother of two boys after all.

But I take comfort in knowing that we make mistakes in order to learn from them and avoid repeating them in the future. This helps us to grow and expand, and to become better versions of ourselves. And as we become these better, upgraded versions, we are able to more readily and easily spread a greater amount of love (encompassing the likes of compassion and kindness and so forth) and joy to those we come in contact with. And in doing so, we inadvertently make ourselves happier as a serendipitous by-product. So even if one were to think about this from a selfish perspective, making others happy ultimately makes us happier within ourselves, which is surely something worth getting behind?

And if we're conscious and aware, we'll have greater clarity of the vision of the full jigsaw puzzle picture as it reveals itself, rather than only finally seeing it in its full glory just before we pass. If we take a close examination of our lives, we will be gifted with the joy of being able to appreciate and revel in the beauty and majesty of the picture as it unfolds.

For those who are ready and want to learn, there already exists an abundance of invaluable information out there in the ether that does a magnificent job of teaching about healing, a huge amount of which is freely available. All it takes is a desire and commitment to learn, implement and practise.

Hence, the purpose of this book is not to act as a manual (although I list some resources that I found useful in the appendix), but simply to act as a flashlight to illuminate this path to anyone not already on it. My hope is that, at the very least, it will provide some inspiration and impetus to some, especially those who are new to personal transformation, to start to get curious and seek information for themselves; that my story will serve as comfort and encouragement to some in the face of challenge and to demonstrate what is possible if we put our hearts and minds into something and take a more elevated perspective.

Healing allows us to move ourselves out of suffering: it helps us to release difficult emotions to make space for more uplifting and joyful ones. What follows is greater happiness and inner peace, which, in turn, enables us to come into the fullness of our being, to live our lives with the greatest expression of who we came here to be.

And in becoming the person we want to be, that we're meant to be, we get to create the most magnificent final puzzle picture possible that is within our power.

CHAPTER 5

ROMANTIC LOVE

Despite my ex-husband's affair, I don't consider myself unlucky in love. I have been fortunate to have experienced my fair share of romantic love throughout my nearly five decades of this life and have been blessed to have shared long-term relationships with some wonderful men.

By now, you'll know that my journey to start mending my heart from the ending of my marriage was a long, windy and undulating one. But eventually, I felt strong enough to start dating again, mainly out of curiosity to see what the dating world was like after such a long time away from it, but also to see what emotions would arise within me in the process. And it was certainly insightful, to say the least.

It wasn't long before I found myself emotionally involved with a chap that I was very taken by. It was all rather exciting, but I'd be lying if I said that it wasn't also somewhat of an emotional rollercoaster ride which provided ample opportunity for fear and doubt to set in. Despite this though, to my surprise, I discovered that I didn't capitulate to my insecurities, which would have been an easy thing to do given my previous heartbreak, and this made me grateful for, and wonder at, my own resolve.

I've always been a very active person and run regularly, for mental and physical health rather than competitively. And I like to treat my runs as meditation practices, utilising the solitude of the exercise to give my thoughts a chance to roam freely. It's almost as if the physical up-and-down motion of my head shakes them into some sort of coherent order and, consequently, I often have mini-epiphanies or insights during these morning runs. In fact, much of this book is made up of entries lifted from my electronic journal that were written after such runs.

One such moment of insight was during the time I was involved with the guy mentioned above, when the following phrases popped into my head during one of my runs:

'Give love like you've never been hurt before.'
'Receive love like you've never felt love before.'

When I pondered the meaning of these thoughts, I understood them to mean the following: the first phrase simply means that despite previous heartbreaks, we humans have the capacity, if we choose to, to give love to others unreservedly, without feeling the need to withhold our love for fear of having our hearts broken again.

And the second phrase means to open our hearts to love so that when someone gives their love, we treat it with reverence and don't take it for granted; we treat each new relationship as if it was our first, untainted by baggage and hurt from previous relationships.

It occurred to me that to live and love by these aspirations requires vast inner strength, courage and bravery. Because as beautiful as romantic love is, nobody can deny that it can come with great emotional pain and stress at times, no matter how the people involved feel for each other.

And whilst I'm not saying that it would necessarily be easy, I can't help but feel that the world would be a better place if we were to aspire to live and love by these codes. What wondrous jigsaw puzzles could partners in romantic relationships create if they were able to love each other more fully, without being impeded by past pain?

Heartache after heartache, if we always choose to still love in this way despite the pain, and consciously choose not to put walls and barriers around us by way of protection, our hearts will expand and grow stronger and make space for even more love. Each time we heal from heartbreak, no matter how minor, we realise how much inner capacity we have to continue loving. We realise we can manage and transcend any pain that may present itself and this then gives us the strength to love courageously.

When we heal ourselves after each hurt, heal our hearts and emotional bodies from the pain of grief from the loss of a relationship, we get stronger and become more whole as individuals, increasing our capacity to love and be loved each time, transforming us into the loving beings that we have the potential to become.

After becoming single again, I remember telling a friend that I wanted to learn to become emotionally stronger. One way of doing this would be through experiences of love and loss, and I certainly got to practise that whilst dating, albeit at a superficial level. And whilst on the face of it, love without associated loss seems like the holy grail for relationships, it's helpful to realise that there will always be loss. Even if we are to find our forever person, one or other individual will die eventually (the hope is always that this would be in the very distant future), so loss is inevitable, and acceptance of this fact should ease the fear of that eventuality.

Also, it's common for us to choose partners when we are in our twenties and thirties with the expectation that these relationships will last us our lifetimes. And for many, it does: the individuals in the relationship are able to grow and evolve together over time in a wonderful union, creating a synergy where the whole becomes greater than the sum of the parts.

But for others, especially given current average life expectancy rates, the expectation for relationships to last over fifty years becomes arguably less realistic or at least far less certain. For many, especially those who choose a path of personal growth, a decade can see profound and significant changes in personality and life perspectives and unless both partners are committed to growing together, there is a likelihood that the trajectory of growth diverges to the point that one or other partner outgrows their relationship.

When we understand this reality, we become less attached to the idea that a relationship needs to last forever to be meaningful, freeing us to enjoy them and be truly appreciative of them in the moment. And if anything, counter-intuitively, not being attached to the idea that the relationship will last forever could potentially incentivise us to make more effort in our relationships. If we are less likely to take our partners for granted than we possibly would if we knew that they were always going to be there, we increase the chances of the relationship staying the course.

For singletons, romantic love or the endeavour to find it shouldn't be something to rush into. Time alone can be invaluably well spent in discovering who we are and nurturing our own inner world so that we become more self-aware and expanded. This enables us to ascertain what's important to us and to know our own value and worth outside of romantic relationships, which makes us better equipped to love more deeply and authentically within romantic relationships.

And what if we've already found someone we believe to be our forever person? For those of us who are fortunate enough to have been in long-term relationships, we know about the honeymoon period and how years into a relationship, it can take effort to keep the embers burning. But instead of allowing familiarity to breed contempt, so to speak, or even for the passing of time to lead to boredom, conscious daily doses of love, (such as little acts of kindness that we know the other will appreciate, being a little more patient if they're doing something that usually gets on our nerves, being gentler if they're winding us up or letting them know we appreciate them for no reason) will provide the kindling to keep the fire alight and prevent the love that's there from going into hibernation.

With each small act of love towards our partner, performed consciously and daily, we build up the reservoir of love between us so that when disagreements invariably arise, there is plenty in reserve to fall back on. Consequently, conflicts don't have the power to build up enough charge to eventually sound the death knell of the relationship.

There are countless teachings available on how to have better relationships, and even conscious, elevated ones too. It's a whole field of study in and of its own so there is little point in my attempting to go into any of that in depth here. My desire here is simply for my words to be a gentle reminder and nudge for couples to consciously be more loving towards each other, and to encourage the utilisation of available resources where appropriate to this end. It's a most fascinating topic!

Huge caveat: none of the above applies where one party in a relationship treats the other abusively. In those situations, get help or get out.

It's funny how our state of mind influences our perspective. Now that I've done sufficient inner work, I can see with a clarity that I didn't possess during those first couple of years, that I was actually harbouring an unacknowledged longing to be in a relationship, borne from the desire to fill an emotional hole in my heart left by the ending of my marriage. Working on self-love and healing my emotional wounds allowed me to see, somewhat paradoxically from noticing the absence of that subconscious longing, that it was even there in the first place.

Realisations like these remind me how life always reveals to us what we need to know if we are patient and wait for the answers to unfold. I have a tendency for impatience at times, often wanting to run before I can walk, eager to understand the purpose or the point of a given situation where clarity is lacking. But experiences like this have given me a sense of knowing that in situations of uncertainty, where the solution, learning or path ahead seem to elude me, if I'm patient, with both myself and with life, then the answers will eventually be revealed as they're meant to, in perfect timing.

Romantic love can be, without a doubt, a most wondrous thing, and we have the capacity to make it more so if we do the work to heal our inner wounds so that we become more whole and complete within us, or if we at the very least take personal responsibility for doing that healing for ourselves.

The more emotionally whole and complete we become and the more love we have for ourselves, the less we'll find that we need to be in a relationship simply as a way to fill an emotional void within us.And thus we are more able to enter into relationships to give love rather than to get love. In giving ourselves the love that we need, we become more able to give that love to others and consequently, relationships can become less transactional and more loving.

In understanding and accepting that other people aren't there to make us happy and that it is our own responsibility to do so, we are rewarded with the realisation that we already have all that we need. Entering into a relationship then becomes a conscious choice, intentionally deciding that the other person is worthy of sharing our time and energy with. We therefore choose a partner knowing that we have much love to offer someone who can be an equally loving contributor in the relationship.

In manifesting a more gorgeous version of our own jigsaw puzzles for ourselves, we develop the potential for an even more gorgeous version of our own and our partner's jigsaw puzzle when we are in a romantic relationship.

Moreover, the more we open our hearts to love in all its many guises, with all of the people in our lives, such that we nurture emotional closeness and connection with our friends and loved ones, the less we need our romantic partners to be the sole provider of this love and connection for us. This frees us to be more loving and giving within our romantic relationships, as we're less focused on what we're expecting the relationship to give us and less attached to the notions of how the relationship should be. We are thus afforded the space and grace to see and appreciate the relationship for what it is, without the veils of our own conditioning and expectations, and those of society.

I've certainly found that the more I know and love myself, and the more time and energy I've invested in nurturing my close friendships and relationships with my loved ones, the less I feel the need to be in a romantic relationship. That's not to say I'm not open to it, simply that I no longer yearn for it as I once did and if I do decide to venture into a romantic relationship, it will be a conscious decision to do so.

However long their duration, all romantic relationships can provide copious amounts of opportunities to practise being more loving, not just the soppy love of the honeymoon period, but also the adult mature love that's needed during inevitable times of disagreement, so that those challenging times become events that deepen and strengthen the relationship rather than create division.

But like parenting, there is no manual for romantic love and nobody teaches us how to have great relationships growing up, other than what we see role modelled by our parents and couples around us, yet we often enter into relationships just expecting them to work well. Even if we are lucky enough to have amazing role models (my parents are a fantastic team, having honed the right level of give and take, with immense respect and care for each other over their fifty-plus years together), we can still greatly enhance our lives by learning how to have empowered and empowering relationships, and learning these invaluable skills has the added benefit of being applicable across all of our relationships, not just romantic ones.

Romantic relationships have the power to test us like no other type of relationship can (apart from possibly parent-child relationships). Nobody can simultaneously make us feel such levels of affection yet so equally wound up the way our partners can. And it's precisely at these moments that we are called to become aware of our emotions and reactions and use them to understand ourselves and our inner landscape, to help us identify areas where we can grow.

And with that growth, we can learn how to choose the higher course of action in a given moment of conflict or disagreement, or at the very least learn how to do the repair work afterwards, even if we have flown off the handle in the heat of the moment. We don't always have to agree with our partners but we can learn to disagree in a productive way that leads to greater understanding of each other and hence nurture closeness and connectedness, rather than building resentment and distance.

It's very rare for romantic relationships to be completely free of conflict or disagreement, but where parties involved are committed to a more loving way of being and to having a conscious relationship, they can eventually reach a point of mutual respect and understanding that allows for a deeper level of love that can transcend the practicalities of life which can cause relationships to stagnate.

If this sounds like hard work, we are invited to get curious as to why we feel this way; to question why we wouldn't want to be putting energy and effort into the thing that forms such an integral and significant part of our lives. If there is fear of it not being reciprocated, then this can be a fair challenge where the other partner is unwilling or unable to do so. But we can only control our own emotions and responses, and articulate our wants and needs in a loving way that the other can understand and relate to. And if sufficient efforts on our part don't elicit a response that honours us, then it is our prerogative to assess the suitability of said relationship. On the other hand though, if the effort is reciprocated, then the love becomes magnified.

In the context of all of this, if we keep our final jigsaw puzzle picture in the back of our minds at all times, then it can aid us to be more loving even when we don't feel like it, when we're tired, when we're in a grump with our partners for something or other, or when there's been a disagreement. It can prompt us to ask ourselves, is it more important that I stay angry at my partner right now just to prove that I'm right, or is it better for the relationship to extend the proverbial olive branch?

It can help us see the bigger picture of what we want for our lives and what we want in our romantic relationships, and hence remind us to not get bogged down during the rough patches.

And as they say, love makes the world go round, and the more conscious we can be in romantic love, the more beautiful our completed puzzle picture will be because of it.

Chapter 6

Personal Growth
and Evolution

Personal growth is about working to become better and, ultimately, the best versions of ourselves over our lifetimes, and so the whole of this book thus far has in essence been about personal growth, from the angles of love in general, self-love, forgiveness and romantic love. Every day of our lives we get the opportunity to practise becoming those better versions, through our interactions with others and internally, to curate our jigsaw puzzles in more positive and loving ways.

Whilst the field of personal growth is immense and available literature immeasurable, this chapter is my interpretation of what I found most valuable in my learning journey over the past three years. I lay this out for anyone interested in going further beyond healing or who are wanting to cultivate a richer personal jigsaw puzzle.

I've already touched upon how our childhood and adolescence impact who we become as adults throughout this book, but it was pivotal in what I learnt about personal growth and so merits drawing out explicitly here.

As children and in our younger years, when we haven't yet developed the emotional maturity or capacity to manage events and emotions in a beneficial way, we develop methods of coping that might have been protective when we were young but become limiting and unhelpful as we get older. These thought patterns and beliefs, in turn, direct our behaviours and form our habits as we grow up.

This conditioning is influenced by everything and everyone that we're exposed to, not just our families but also our friends, teachers, media consumption and so on. The child who is ridiculed in class for answering a question incorrectly can become the adult who doesn't speak up in meetings for fear of saying the wrong thing and looking stupid. The child who experiences tragedy can become the adult who is super cautious and hypervigilant, expecting danger everywhere they turn.

By the time we're adults, we behave in ways that we identify as representative of who we are, as our personalities, not necessarily realising that the reality is simply that those behaviours have been directed by patterns and beliefs formed through childhood and early life conditioning and we're just acting them out unconsciously.

For a long time, it was believed that the adult brain couldn't change, leading many people to accept their thoughts and behaviours as unalterable, hence the use of phrases such as, *It's just the way I am* or *You can't teach an old dog new tricks*. However, neuroscience has since shown that our brains are elastic and have the ability to create new synapses and new circuitry if given the appropriate environment and training (referred to as neuroplasticity), bringing about the ability to develop new behaviours given sufficient time.

In understanding this, we realise that we have the power to change any limiting beliefs and thought patterns that don't serve us and thus we gain the potential to change ourselves for the better - we have the potential for personal growth, should we choose it.

When faced with challenges, no matter how big or small, whilst we often can't control the challenge itself, we still always have a choice over our response. We can either blame the people or circumstances that we think are making us feel our unwanted feelings, *They shouldn't have done this* or *They shouldn't have said that* or *That shouldn't have happened*, or we can take responsibility for the way we're thinking, feeling and reacting to the given situation.

If we do the former, we become victims, trapped by our circumstances and a prisoner of our thoughts and emotions. But when we understand that our limiting beliefs are just those acquired from childhood and hence don't have to dictate our behaviour, we can choose the latter course of action: we can choose to learn to do something more empowering for ourselves and it's from this that we can then grow. An old dog can most definitely be taught new tricks. It might take longer for older people, but that's no reason not to try.

Personal growth is available to each and every one of us, regardless of our age, if we wish for it. Some people live their entire lives not realising how much agency they have over their own thoughts and emotions, and so they feel that life just happens to them with little they can do about it. And there's nothing wrong with that - it's not for anyone to judge how another lives their life. And they're right in the sense that sometimes things in life happen that you can do nothing about. But in knowing that we can direct our thinking and feelings by changing our perspective, we can strengthen our ability to govern the impact those events will have on us, allowing us to live a life of much more ease and grace.

Personal growth doesn't mean that we have to completely overhaul who we are. Most adults are already decent people with many redeeming qualities that their upbringing will have imbued them with, and needless to say, these should be retained.

However, even the best of us will have parts that might not be entirely desirable or beneficial, which sometimes cause conflict or discomfort in our lives, either internally or externally, in our relationships with others or with ourselves. If we have the humility and are willing to accept that this is the case, we have the capacity to change ourselves for the better. And in doing so, piece by piece, section by section, our jigsaw puzzles are assembled more luminously.

And thus personal growth sometimes comes in the form of evolution, small and gradual tweaks over time, rather than large-scale overt changes, and this is especially true in later life when we've acquired plenty of life experience and we're more or less emotionally mature.

For instance, fundamentally I haven't changed all that much from when I embarked on this journey three years ago. I still retain the strong morals, values and ethics that my parents ingrained into us as kids, but I had a lot of limiting beliefs and inhibitions that caused me internal anxiety and discomfort as well as hang-ups. As such, much of my personal growth journey so far has been about letting go of the parts of me that weren't serving me or others.

I expect this is the case for most people. It's not that we need to necessarily acquire new qualities but to shed our existing disempowering ones. And in doing so, we find that we naturally acquire more empowering new ones as a happy by-product. For instance, if a person is pessimistic because their childhood was filled with adverse events and negativity, if they are able to work through this and learn to see the good things in their life or come to know that they have the power to bring good things into their life, then slowly, that pessimism can naturally turn into optimism and hence bring a more hopeful outlook.

Even someone with the most idyllic childhood isn't necessarily immune from the need for personal growth, because for them, lack of adversity or challenge in younger life might result in them not developing mental and emotional resilience to cope with trauma or adversity in their adult life. There is truth in the old adage that what doesn't kill you makes you stronger. We need to believe and know that we have the capacity to endure. Being faced with and overcoming adversity builds mental and emotional toughness. So if that adversity comes later in life, it might precipitate the need to develop the agency to overcome and transcend challenges. And thus personal growth is still relevant, powerful and empowering.

To choose to intentionally and consciously pursue personal growth is the greatest gift a person can give oneself. Because through personal growth, over time we gradually free ourselves of the self-imposed shackles of limiting beliefs and patterns of behaviour that hold us down and tie us to our thoughts and emotions.

Each time we rid ourselves of a belief or behaviour pattern that doesn't serve us, we sever one of those chains that binds us, and progressively we give ourselves the gift of liberation: freedom from the torment of our own disempowering and repressive thoughts, and freedom from feeling weighed down by our own uncomfortable emotions.

And with that liberation comes the capacity to live our lives with passion and joy, to have the courage to express ourselves fully and reach our full potential, and to bring our gifts and our love and light to the world.

But pursuing personal growth isn't an easy endeavour; it requires dedication and diligence and calls for us to become deeply intimate with ourselves. By that, I mean it requires us to spend time, some of it in solitude, with our own thoughts and emotions, getting to know ourselves as intimately as we would a lover. And critically, it requires us to become brutally honest with ourselves, so that we learn to understand our thought patterns and our habits.

Now you might be thinking, *I already know myself and am already honest with myself.* And that might be true, but for most, if not all of us, there will be parts of us that are subtly hidden.

As an example, I was a sensitive child and took criticism, or what I perceived to be criticism, extremely personally. Simply through the innocent lack of understanding on my parents' part, I wasn't equipped with the tools to manage this, so I developed my own coping mechanism to protect myself so that criticisms wouldn't hurt me. I adopted a tough exterior to compensate for my sensitive nature and constructed shields of defensiveness to deflect the arrows of hurtful comments or opinions. I did this by telling myself that I was fine, that I wasn't bothered about what was said when deep down I was undoubtedly affected.

One day, after I'd started learning about this subject, a friend was telling me about a problem that was troubling her and even though I could see it was clearly bothering her, she went on to say that she was fine. And it was only then that I realised that this is exactly what I myself did. It seems a little silly now that I'm writing it, but I'd done it so many times throughout my whole life that I no longer even noticed that I was doing it. It was quite a lightbulb moment for me.

After that, I became more aware and started to notice and catch myself. Every time I said *I'm fine* or *It's fine,* I'd stop and circle back. I got curious, I dug deeper. I started questioning myself. *Come on Hanh, you're not fine. What's the matter?* When I confronted myself like this, I would find that I was actually really upset or annoyed by the thing that had been said and was just telling myself that I wasn't to prevent it from bothering me. I would then go further and question why I was so bothered by it and would discover that it was usually because something I was believing about myself or the situation was causing me to interpret what had been said as a personal attack. I would then go on to counsel myself to reframe what had been said (*maybe they were having a bad day,* or *I'm sure they didn't mean it like that*), to depersonalise it, to shift my own perception of it being a criticism directed at me to simply a comment. And in doing so, I was able to stop myself from ruminating on what had been said.

It's been a process rather than an overnight change and I'm not completely there yet, but now, when I catch myself thinking *It's fine,* more often than not, it really is fine. Just like our jigsaw puzzles, our lives are an ongoing work in progress.

In essence, the inner work that we need to do for our own personal growth is to notice when we've been triggered. In other words, notice when something someone said or did has caused us to have an adverse reaction, and use that as a pointer for something we can grow from. For instance, if we find ourselves feeling jealous (assuming we're not being deliberately provoked into it), we can get curious about where this is coming from. Does it stem from an insecure attachment to our caretakers as children, causing us to feel not good enough? If so, inner work can be carried out on this belief of inadequacy, and whilst it might not eradicate feelings of jealousy altogether, it can foster a more empowered way of managing it when it arises as well as lessening it over time.

But not everything that irks us has its origins from childhood, or not in an obvious way at least. And changing our behaviour is typically much easier said than done, and once we're older and are having to fight against decades of habits, it can be slow-going.

For example, as a non-driver, I've always walked wherever possible throughout my entire adult life and so habituated to a fast pace early on, partly to minimise travel time and partly because I use it as a means of exercise. But with that fast pace came impatience. There was a time when I would feel annoyed with people walking slowly on the pavement and I would overtake them. I wouldn't express my annoyance outwardly, but internally it would be there. One day, a couple of years ago, I found myself feeling irritated with someone who was ambling along the pavement just ahead of me and so I overtook them, as usual. But after doing so, because I was present and aware, I caught myself and asked, *Hanh, why are you in such a rush? You don't need to be anywhere right now.* I realised that I was in such a habit of rushing that it had become my default, unconscious, behaviour.

I knew that this part of me didn't serve me or anyone else, so I decided to change it by altering my perception. Previously, I was getting annoyed with the amblers because I thought they were being slow, but once I could see that my annoyance stemmed solely from my own impatience, rather than their slowness, I was able to start the work to overcome my irritation. It wasn't an instantaneous change; I still had to remind myself several times to begin with but now, whilst I still overtake people if they're walking slower than I am, I do so without my previous annoyance. And now I usually give them a little smile as I walk past. But I'm not perfect and occasionally when things are weighing on my mind, I might slip back into old habits and charge past a fellow pedestrian, but these times serve as reminders for the next.

But the objective of personal growth isn't about eradicating all of our less desirable thoughts or emotions, as this would be an insurmountable endeavour indeed. Thoughts pop into our heads all the time without our control, but that doesn't mean that we need to identify with them as being ours. When we understand that all of our unconscious thoughts are shaped by our life conditioning, we can choose to learn to become a witness to them and let them go if they don't serve us.

For instance, judgemental or critical thoughts about myself or others still pop into my head unconsciously and may linger there or lead onto other unhelpful trains of thought, especially if I'm sleep deprived, haven't eaten well or my hormones are imbalanced. But when I'm present, I am able to notice them, recognise that they are just unconscious thoughts and then consciously correct my thinking to something kinder or more loving. It's not that I'm dismissing or bypassing my thoughts, I'm just choosing not to identify with them.

Our brains are naturally wired to look for signs of danger or fault, especially when we're feeling under stress. Knowing this allows us to have compassion for ourselves when we have negative or unhelpful thoughts. There's nothing wrong with us, we're not being negative, it's just our innate biology. It also means that we can consciously choose not to jump on those thought trains.

It's similar with emotions although not quite the same, the subtle difference being that our emotional states certainly and most definitely do matter, and thus it's of vital importance that we acknowledge them rather than suppress or bypass them. But having done so, we can still choose to reframe our perspective so that we can feel our emotions in a more productive or helpful way.

For instance, nervousness and excitement have virtually identical physiological responses, such as elevated heart rates and cortisol levels (the stress response hormone), but we experience them differently based on our conditioning. So, as an example, if we felt nervousness as a child just before a race and then went on to lose that race, we might come to associate that nervousness with fear of losing and hence nervousness could become a debilitating emotion. But if we went on to win that race, we might then associate that nervousness with the excitement of the prospect of winning, and hence it becomes an enjoyable emotion for us to experience.

This is a simplistic example but it illustrates how an emotion can be felt differently depending on how it's perceived. And whilst the perception for the child here was dictated by the circumstances, as adults we can create this reframing of our emotions for ourselves to help us experience them in a more empowered way.

So, by becoming aware of our thoughts and emotions and being present, we can alter our reactions to them to be more loving responses rather than our habitual or impulsive reactions. When someone pulls out in front of us, our unconscious initial thought might still be an exasperated, *What on earth are these so-and-sos doing?* but instead of then interpreting it as a personal slight and following it up with associated anger, we can choose to give them the benefit of the doubt that they didn't see us.

Sometimes, when I'm finding everything a bit too much as a single mum, my thoughts can veer towards the road of frustration, at the fact that when I chose to have children, I never planned to be bringing them up mostly by myself. But I have the presence of mind to catch my thoughts and guide myself, to not stray down that road as it will only lead to a dark and inhospitable place. So I take a pause, reset and find a more illuminated road, one that will lead to a more inviting and inspiring location.

But personal growth doesn't always have to be so serious. It can be a lot of fun too if we keep our minds open to the possibility of learning new things at whatever stage in our lives, as I was lucky enough to do last winter. Having been an avid snowboarder for nine years before having children, during our family ski trip I decided to swap my board for skis in an attempt to try something new and had lessons with my boys as a complete novice.

I felt quite clumsy with my skis and poles and it did occur to me how much easier it would have been to have stuck with my board, but I was committed to learning and wanted to share this experience with my boys, and so I persevered. And I was rewarded not only with the exhilaration of learning a new skill but also having a blast with my children.

Neuroscience has shown that our brains have the ability to grow new brain cells when we learn new things, through a process called neurogenesis, thus in doing so we help protect our brains from cognitive decline. And learning new things can be as simple as doing things with our non-dominant hand, for example, or taking a new route to work or cooking a new recipe. The minutiae of life need not be mundane and can provide ample opportunities to learn if we look closely and adopt a growth mindset.

The paths to personal growth are many and varied. It matters less how we go about it than that we choose to do it. Life provides us with challenges to test our mettle, to push us to become better, for ourselves, for our loved ones and for the collective human race.

The saying goes, 'Live each day like it's your last,' but I prefer to think that we should live each day like it's our first, where we possess the curiosity of a child, unjaded by the mundanity of adult life, eager to see what we can learn today and keen to appreciate the beauty of nature and those around us. Adopting a beginner's mind, as per Zen Buddhist philosophy, and a growth mindset allows for an openness and receptiveness to what life offers.

For sure there will be times when we won't feel like learning, where fatigue steers us to comfort and the familiar. And on these days we need to be compassionate with ourselves and honour that and just be, relaxing into the fullness of our lives, often hectic, sometimes messy and chaotic, but ultimately ours to make of what we will. And thus our jigsaw puzzles build up organically, majestically, as we open up to the natural flow of life.

As we grow and evolve, we find a life balance that works for us, our own personal exquisite dance between activity and rest, dark and light, company and solitude. When we stay in any extremes for too long, we become out of balance. From a physiological perspective, our bodies always want to get back to homeostasis where all our bodily systems are in balance, for optimum functioning. For instance, if we're too hot we'll naturally want to do something to cool down and vice versa. In extending the definition of homeostasis to include our mental and emotional systems, we realise that not only is it okay to relax amidst all of our doing and achieving but that it's actually necessary in order to reach balance, and thus create homeostasis for ourselves holistically.

An important point to note with regard to personal growth is that in a world of skewed images of perfection perpetuated by social media, it is helpful to understand that perfection is a false goal for life which cannot be achieved. We are all flawed in our own unique way, but there is perfection in our imperfections and aiming to meet other people's expectations or comparing ourselves to curated images of others is not helpful for our self-growth. In running our own race, staying in our own lane without worrying about how others are doing, we can focus on our distinct merits and improvements and hence appreciate how far we've come on our personal journey. Assessing our progress against our own unique yardstick is the only accurate measure of how we're doing.

At its core, personal growth is an act of love; love towards ourselves through the liberation from our own limiting beliefs and thoughts and emotions that don't serve us, and love towards others through becoming better partners/parents/family members/friends. We all have the power to become higher versions of ourselves if we choose to, if we put love at the heart of what we do and have the courage and conviction to do so.

The more mindful and conscious we become of how we want our individual completed jigsaw puzzles to look, the more intentional we can become with how we live our lives. And thus, we can all be artists creating beautifully exquisite masterpieces that we call our lives, and for our efforts, we are handsomely rewarded with life experiences rich with meaning, purpose and joy.

CHAPTER 7

WEALTH - AN ALTERNATIVE DEFINITION

This chapter might seem incongruent with the rest of this book so far, and thus a little out of place, but as this book is about love in its broadest scope and in all of its forms, here I take a simplistic look at the topic of wealth through the lens of love.

Money and wealth are very emotive subjects and hence anyone's personal subjective opinion can have the potential to cause offence to at least someone or other, be they lacking in money, or have it in abundance. I include my own viewpoint here as it is relevant in the context of our completed puzzle picture, and my opinions are meant as food for thought, rather than judgements on how others live their lives. My aim is not to dictate to anyone what they should or shouldn't do, but merely to offer an alternative vantage point.

In the modern world, much emphasis is placed on material success and achievement. Whilst these things are not unimportant and have, without a doubt, been the motivation for a great many accomplishments that have benefitted vast numbers of people over time, as the developed world grows wealthier and wealthier, we're beginning to see that this emphasis has started to come at the expense of, amongst other things, people's mental and emotional health.

To be clear, I am as much of a fan of money as the next person, appreciating it as a tool that enables us to live comfortably and enjoy wonderful experiences, acutely aware of its power to buy us the freedom to do what we want with our time. But I think the definition of wealth that has served the modern world so well for so long is in need of review. So far, wealth in developed societies has been measured by the number of zeros at the end of a person's bank balance and I think that the time has come for a change in this perception. This isn't new - I've heard similar thoughts discussed on a couple of recent podcasts and here I'm adding my voice to the call, with my own personal interpretation.

What if, instead of measuring a person's wealth solely by the amount of money a person has, we were to also include the amount of happiness a person is able to bring into other people's lives, as well as how much true, inner joy a person has within themselves? Granted, as a statistician, I appreciate that this would be incredibly difficult to measure, but that shouldn't be a reason for not making this something for people to aspire to or strive for.

I studied economics at school and as part of my degree, so I understand the boundless complexities involved in how economies operate. Therefore, I am not so naive to think that there exists a simple solution for a fairer distribution of money and wealth, or an easy way to reduce the number of people in financial need. So that's not what I'm advocating here.

In essence, I believe that change can happen if people become more conscious about what they do with their financial wealth. If those who can spare it were to use their wealth to help others, would it not bring benefits for them too? Warm clothes bought for those in need using charitable donations would indeed warm the bodies of the recipients, but would knowing that a fellow human had been aided not also warm the hearts of the donors themselves? Similarly, wouldn't meals bought for those without sufficient food not only fill their bellies but also fill the hearts of those who had provided funding to fulfil this need?

If we were to change our general definition of wealth away from the purely material of the present day, to incorporate more intangible elements such as kindness, care and charity, what would that look like? How would this change to the definition of wealth impact the jigsaw puzzles of people across the world?

What if we included the happiness that doesn't need money to generate, such as the joy a loving parent can gift to their children, the care a person can provide for a pet, or the wisdom that an elder can freely and lovingly impart to younger generations? When we think about it like this, the possibilities to raise one's wealth through this adapted definition become endless.

If more of the people with more zeros on the end of their bank balance were to help those with fewer zeros, what could be achieved? And if we were to include those intangibles in the definition of wealth as I've outlined, what would the *World's Richest* list look like? Would it look vastly different to how it does today?

And if we were to take these questions wider, from beyond the individual to companies, how would things look there? Which companies would be at the top of that rich list? And what if we were to expand wider still? If a nation's wealth were to be measured not solely by its GDP, but also by the happiness and general well-being of its citizens, I suspect global wealth tables would look rather different to what they do today.

If we were to start now to change our thinking to a more inclusive definition of wealth, how long would it take for us to see any material positive changes and what would those changes look like? I appreciate that all this sounds like pie-in-the-sky, away-with-the-fairies thinking, but in a world where we can jettison its inhabitants beyond its atmosphere and reach the moon, surely it's not beyond reality? And yes, maybe it might never happen, maybe nothing will change, maybe the complexities of real life will just dictate that the world carries on as it is.

But what if the idea catches fire? What if younger or future generations take to the notion and run with it, and use their creativity and passion to manifest ways to bring about societal changes that see economics and economies evolve to become fairer, so that those at the top of the chain leave more for those at the bottom? In the wild, even the mighty lion, the king of the jungle, having had its fair share of the spoils will leave the rest for others to feast on. Is this something the lions of our society could emulate?

When I was young, we never went upstairs on the bus because that's where smoking was permitted, making it difficult to breathe properly, and in my twenties, coming home from the pub meant reeking of cigarette smoke. This was just the norm, how things were, and you didn't consider it being any different. Yet less than a couple of decades later, there are very few places where smoking is still allowed. And it's even more striking when you take into account that smoking was actively encouraged only several decades before that. This isn't to single out smoking, merely an example of how societal changes can be implemented in a relatively short space of time given the right impetus and conditions.

I appreciate that smoking is a very simplistic example but my point is that big changes that seem unperceivable at one point in time can be brought about with the right catalyst. In the case of smoking, it was people's health. Maybe in the case of the definition of wealth, it will be people's happiness and well-being?

I know that a great many of the wealthy already make sizeable charitable donations, so this is not to overlook that generosity, but it feels like there is still more to do, especially given that there are people, even in a country as rich as ours, who don't have enough to eat. I'm not saying that I have the answers - I don't know any more than the next person what needs to be done, but I know that there are people out there whose intelligence and creativity are far superior to mine, and so my hope in writing this is that the message gets to where it needs to go, and inspires and encourages the right people to take action to create positive change.

If we can find ways to use the vast amounts of money that are generated in developed economies to increase well-being and reduce suffering for society as a whole rather than simply making the rich even richer, we will be able to increase the amount of collective joy in our communities, our towns and cities, throughout countries and across our entire planet.

Change doesn't happen simply through words, it happens when words get put into action. If sufficient individuals take up the mantle to create a critical mass, then collectively a paradigm shift can be generated. The time has come for the paradigm of wealth to be shifted. And shifts of such magnitude require time, and the sooner we start, the sooner change will occur. But it's up to individuals to want to see change. It's up to individuals to consciously consider their own jigsaw puzzles and have a desire and intention to craft them in a way that not only brings them more meaning, purpose and joy, but also contributes to a more glorious universal collective puzzle picture.

CHAPTER 8

THE FINAL PIECE

There is no blueprint for how to live a dream life. Life is inherently messy, profoundly nuanced and intricately complex, but all perfectly so. All the books in the world can guide and assist us, but it's the living and direct experience that will ultimately teach us. If you've never eaten a peach before, you can't know how it tastes just from someone's description of it alone. It's in the doing and being that we learn about ourselves, what we like and don't like, what's important to us and where we want to spend our time and energy.

And it's through making our own mistakes and facing our own challenges that we learn and grow. Nobody can walk this path for us, and acceptance of this sets us free from wishing it were any different, especially in times of challenge. Even the best of us will have good times when we're winning at life and other times when we feel like we're floundering and fumbling through, and sometimes this can happen all in the same day. But in learning to take the rough with the smooth, we condition ourselves to ride the bumps; just like when flying on a plane and turbulence is encountered, the seat belt sign comes on, signalling us to buckle up until we've flown through the agitated air, back to calmer skies.

Generally, when we can get clear on who we are and what is important to us in our own life, we can follow our own North Star and not get sidetracked or derailed by what other people are doing or what we think we should be doing. Or at least not as easily. There may be occasions when we go a little off course, when the currents or winds are strong, but if we hold true to where we're heading and where we want to get to, we'll be able to notice that we're off track and steady the ship back on course.

Equally though, life does not run in a straight line and requires us to be flexible. We might have a general trajectory of where we're heading and sometimes, something massive will throw us completely off course and we realise that, that's life's way of showing us we have a better route to follow. Or we might simply have a change of mind or heart part way through and decide that what we thought we wanted earlier in life no longer holds the same allure, and so we pivot.

But sometimes our North Star isn't a destination, defined by the things we want to achieve. It might simply be a state of being. Maybe our North Star is to live a more meaningful and purposeful life, an aspiration to live more authentically. And living authentically doesn't mean succumbing to all our whims and impulses. Authenticity is found when our words and actions are aligned with our principles and values, even if in the moment our impulses dictate otherwise. Arguably, this is particularly when so, given that our impulses are usually a result of our conditioning.

To live authentically requires virtue and integrity, both of which are exercised not by what we say and who we think we are when life is easy, comfortable and unchallenging, but by how we

84

respond when provoked by others and events beyond our control. It matters less what we say out loud publicly, and more who we are and what we do when there's nobody there to give us praise for it. To talk the talk is easy, but it's in walking the walk that we get to practise flexing our muscles of authenticity and integrity.

Every day, we are given opportunities to practise what we preach. So to preach a higher, more elevated message forces us to ask more of ourselves, to become our better selves and to aspire to a richer life experience.

If this provokes a feeling of resistance within us, get curious and ask why. What is the underlying belief that causes us to turn away from challenging ourselves? If it's a fear of messing up, of not being able to reach our goals, take comfort in knowing that life will catch you, that just like an actual jigsaw puzzle, each piece of your life jigsaw puzzle is shaped to slot perfectly into place with all the others. And if we slip up, we pick ourselves up, dust ourselves off, forgive ourselves and understand that we can endure. As the saying goes, there are no mistakes, only opportunities to learn.

When we find ourselves caught up in the complexities and challenges of modern life and feel overwhelmed, wondering why certain things are happening or why we're feeling a certain way, we can step back from it all. We can surrender to that knowledge and be reassured that even though we might not know what's ahead of us, we can trust that eventually, however long we have, all our jigsaw puzzle pieces are designed to fit together perfectly. And in the end, all the billions of pieces will fit together exactly as they're supposed to, to compose the final and complete picture.

We are each given the gift of life to explore and define, for us to curate into whatever masterpiece we want for ourselves. And whatever that looks like for an individual, if we always put love at the heart of what we choose to do, then our completed jigsaw puzzle picture will be universally captivating.

And even if we do encounter the odd missing piece along the way, it doesn't make the rest of the puzzle invalid or worthless. If we widen our focus to view the picture in its entirety, rather than just zooming in on the pieces that are missing, we can still experience the joy of admiring the exquisiteness of the whole of the puzzle as it slowly unfolds.

I started writing this book in the hope that it would help others see that they can face their challenges in a more empowered and liberating way. But as it unfolded, I came to realise that it has become a gift and a reminder for myself as much as anything, to remind me to keep going back to my own puzzle; to keep reflecting on it and continue to fit the pieces together from a loving perspective, especially when times feel tough.

None of us knows how long we've got in this lifetime and thus we don't know how big our jigsaw puzzle is going to end up. But if we're conscious of curating it as masterfully as we can each and every day, it will be magnificent irrespective of the final number of pieces.

So to conclude, with all of the above in mind, I leave you, dear reader, with a question to ponder over for yourself. With the ability to choose, what would you like your final jigsaw puzzle picture to look like?

Appendix

Here I list a selection of the modalities/resources that I've found helpful in my learning journey so far. I have no affiliation with any of the people mentioned or the links shared, and I'm not advocating them as necessarily effective for everyone. These are simply suggestions for tools and information that can be tried readily and freely.

Personal Growth & Inner Work:

- Soundstrue.com - Insights at the Edge podcast
- Dr. Chatterjee podcast
- The School of Life (website & YouTube channel)
- Lewis Howes podcast
- The Heal podcast
- Internal Family Systems (Richard Schwartz)
- Attachment Theory
- Rapid Transformational Therapy (Marissa Peer)
- Dan Siegel (better parenting through healing oneself)
- Joe Dizpenza (in particular, heart brain coherence)
- Risingwoman.com (inner child work)

Wellness Practices:

- **Qigong:**
  - **https://www.springforestqigong.com/**
  - **https://www.holdenqigong.com/**

- **Meditation:**

  There are far too many to list here and different types of meditation can be used for different purposes. My recommendation is to try some guided ones on YouTube, depending on what your need is and see how they resonate with you. In time, you'll ascertain the ones that work for you.

- **Yoga:**

  Sue Morter BodyAwake Yoga (search YouTube).

  Brett Larkin Yoga (search YouTube)

NERVOUS SYSTEM REGULATION:

The workings of the nervous system deserve to be understood in greater detail than I can do the subject justice here, so I will assume that the reader has basic knowledge of how it works. It is well known that exercise, sufficient quality sleep, a healthy diet, connection with others and time spent in nature can help us regulate our nervous system, as can techniques such as meditation and Qigong. But in the heat of the moment, we might need tools that can move us quickly away from our stress response. Here are a couple:

- **Tapping or EFT (Emotional Freedom Technique):**
  - https://www.thetappingsolution.com/
- **Physiological Sigh:**
  - https://governmentscienceandengineering.blog.gov.uk/2021/11/26/is-a-sigh-just-a-sigh/
  - https://www.youtube.com/watch?v=rBdhqBGqiMc

ACKNOWLEDGEMENTS

My boys, Elliot and Blake, are my greatest teachers, pushing me daily to grow my muscles of patience, compassion and kindness. They are unintentionally tough taskmasters, challenging me continually to be a better parent. And when I mess up, they are forgiving and unconditional with their love. Without them, my world would be less colourful and I would be a lesser person. Thank you, boys.

Thank you to my wonderful and selfless parents who have taught me so much and have done so much for me. I wouldn't be where, or who, I am today without you. And to all my amazing siblings, thank you for being my ready-made friends and companions throughout my life. It is my great fortune and honour to have you as my family.

Faye and Wing were my confidantes when I needed to mentally and emotionally download in the difficult early days. Thank you, girls, for showing up, being present and helping me stay sane!

Olly, Brian and Rosie, thank you for being guinea pigs and beta-readers. Your supportive and valuable feedback has been greatly appreciated.

And lastly, this book would not exist without Simon. Thank you for your permission and support in writing this book, and for our brilliant children. They say things happen for a reason, and the reason is always for our highest good. Our marriage might have ended but our joint love for our children and our friendship will endure.

-o-

Along my journey over the past three years, I have been blessed by the teachings and works of many whom I've never met before and who are unaware of my existence. Their content has been invaluable and inspiring, for which I have much deep-felt gratitude. Whilst this list is far from exhaustive, my sincere thanks go out to the following people who have been and remain influential in my learning:

- **Christina Lopes** - my first Spirituality teacher.
- **Aaron Abke** - deepened my Spiritual understanding.
- **Nicky Sutton** - supported my Spiritual awakening.
- **Tami Simon,** Sounds True founder - provider of too many profoundly valuable podcast episodes to list.
- **Dr Rangan Chatterjee** - another resource of wonderfully insightful podcasts.
- **Master Chunyi Lin** - Spring Forest Qigong master.
- **Lee Holden** - my other (equally inspiring) Qigong master.
- **Dr Sue Morter** - BodyAwake yoga and energy healing guru.
- **Alex Howard** - nervous system reset and emotional healing mentor.
- **The Ortner family,** founders of The Tapping Solution - helped calm my nervous system down when I really needed it.
- **Dr Shefali Tsabary** - my first guide to conscious parenting.

Author's Notes

I've read and heard so many quotes and teachings in my time, and similar messages told by different people, that quite often I can't remember exactly who to attribute them to, so in this book, I haven't attempted to do so, for the avoidance of error.

-o-

For anyone familiar with spirituality and has picked up the spiritual undertones in my work, that is because spirituality is central to my life, and is what guided me to write this book in the first place. But I have deliberately written it from a non-spiritual perspective, not from a denial of my spiritual beliefs, but because I wanted to spread the message of greater love, which is the core of spirituality, to as many people as possible. I wanted it to be relevant to the mums on the school run and to anyone who is either unaware of spirituality or finds it 'woo-woo'. The purpose of my book is simply to help spread love and light to anyone who might be in need of encouragement during tough times and to use what I learnt from the challenges that I went through to be of service to others. The Universe will guide individuals to their own awakening in divine timing.

-o-

After completing my book and whilst getting it ready for publication, I decided it would be a good idea to search the internet for my chosen book title just to make sure that it hadn't already been used. And whilst I didn't find any reference to the exact title that I had chosen, I did find some articles (which I was previously unaware of) around the topic of using jigsaw puzzles as an analogy for life. So I felt it important to assert that my account of how the idea of this book and its jigsaw puzzle analogy came to me, as described in the *Introduction*, is true and accurate, and any similarities to articles on the subject are purely coincidental and sincerely unintentional. On the one hand, I guess I should have searched for my book title earlier on in the process (!), but such is the naivety of a first-time indie writer. But on the other hand, if I had done that, there's a chance that it would have deterred me from writing this book in the first place, preventing its materialisation, so for that, I'm glad I didn't.

ABOUT THE AUTHOR

Of Chinese ethnicity and born in Vietnam, Hanh came to the UK at the tender age of four and grew up in Sheffield before moving away for university. She made London her home following graduation, where she still lives with her two sons, Elliot and Blake, a ten-minute walk from their dad's home. In the summer of 2023, after twenty-six rewarding years working in IT, she decided that it was time to try a different flavour of life, leaving her corporate job in order to go on new adventures and see where life takes her.

Find out more about her and get in touch at: **www.hanhtat.com**

Printed in Great Britain
by Amazon